ANATOLIA
IN THE SECOND MILLENNIUM B.C.

BY

MAURITS N. VAN LOON

With 46 plates

LEIDEN
E. J. BRILL
1985

ISBN 90 04 07105 9

ANATOLIA IN
THE SECOND MILLENNIUM B.C.

INSTITUTE OF RELIGIOUS ICONOGRAPHY
STATE UNIVERSITY GRONINGEN

ICONOGRAPHY OF RELIGIONS

EDITED BY

Th. van Baaren, L. P. van den Bosch, L. Leertouwer, F. Leemhuis
H. te Velde, H. Witte, and H. Buning (*Secretary*)

SECTION XV: MESOPOTAMIA AND THE NEAR EAST

FASCICLE TWELVE

LEIDEN
E. J. BRILL
1985

CONTENTS

ABBREVIATIONS AND BIBLIOGRAPHY

ABBREVIATIONS

AAAO	FRANKFORT, H., *The Art and Architecture of the Ancient Orient*, Harmondsworth 1954.
AfO	*Archiv für Orientforschung.*
AG	ÖZGÜÇ, N., *The Anatolian Group of Cylinder Seal Impressions from Kültepe* (TTKY V:22), Ankara 1965.
AJA	*American Journal of Archaeology.*
ALF	EMRE, K., *Anatolian Lead Figurines and their Stone Moulds* (TTKY VI:14), Ankara 1971.
Der Alte Orient	ORTHMANN, W., ed., *Propyläen Kunstgeschichte 14: Der Alte Orient*, Berlin 1975.
AnatSt	*Anatolian Studies.*
Ancient Art	MUSCARELLA, O. W., ed., *Ancient Art: The Norbert Schimmel Collection*, Mainz 1974.
ANET³	PRITCHARD, J. B., ed., *Ancient Near Eastern Texts*, 3rd ed., Princeton 1969.
BAK	BOEHMER. R. M. & H. HAUPTMANN, eds., *Beiträge zur Altertumskunde Kleinasiens: Festschrift für Kurt Bittel*, Mainz 1983.
CANES I	PORADA, E., ed., *Corpus of Ancient Near Eastern Seals in North American Collections I: The Collection of the Pierpont Morgan Library*, Washington 1948.
Les Hittites	BITTEL, K., *Les Hittites* (L'Univers des Formes), Paris 1976.
HFY	BITTEL, K., et al., *Das hethitische Felsheiligtum Yazilikaya*, Berlin 1975.
IstMitt	*Istanbuler Mitteilungen.*
JCS	*Journal of Cuneiform Studies.*
JKF	*Jahrbuch für Kleinasiatische Forschung.*
JNES	*Journal of Near Eastern Studies.*
KAF	HROUDA, B., *Die Kulturgeschichte des assyrischen Flachbildes*, Bonn 1965.
Kleinasien	GOETZE, A., *Kleinasien* (Handbuch der Altertumswissenschaft III.1.3.3.1, 2nd ed.), Munich 1957.
MAW	KRAMER, S. N., ed., *Mythologies of the Ancient World*, Garden City, N.Y. 1961.
MDOG	*Mitteilungen der Deutschen Orient-Gesellschaft.*
MIO	*Mitteilungen des Instituts für Orientforschung.*
MMJ	*Metropolitan Museum Journal.*
MUSJ	*Mélanges de l'Université Saint-Joseph.*
MVAeG	Mitteilungen der Vorderasiatisch-Aegyptischen Gesellschaft.
NDH	LAROCHE, E., *Recherches sur les noms des dieux hittites*, Paris 1947.
OIP	Oriental Institute Publications.
OLZ	*Orientalistische Literatur-Zeitung.*
RA	*Revue d'Assyriologie.*
RHA	*Revue Hittite et Asianique.*
RLA	EBELING, E., et al., eds., *Reallexikon der Assyriologie*, Berlin 1928-.
SAOC	Studies in Ancient Oriental Civilization.
TAD	*Türk Arkeoloji Dergisi.*
TTKY	Türk Tarih Kurumu Yayinlari.
Ugaritica III	SCHAEFFER, C. F. A., *Ugaritica III* (Mission de Ras Shamra 8), Paris 1956.
WVDOG	Wissenschaftliche Veröffentlichungen der Deutschen Orient-Gesellschaft.
WZKM	*Wiener Zeitschrift für die Kunde des Morgenlandes.*
ZA	*Zeitschrift für Assyriologie.*

BIBLIOGRAPHY

AKURGAL, E., *Die Kunst der Hethiter*, Munich 1961, pp. 18-89.
ALEXANDER, R. L., *The Mountain-God at Eflâtun Pinar*, Anatolica 2, Leiden 1968, pp. 77-86.
——, *The Signe Royal at Fraktin*, JNES 36, Chicago 1977, pp. 199-207.
——, *The Tyszkiewicz Group of Stamp Cylinders*, Anatolica 5, Leiden 1973-76, pp. 141-215.

ALP, S., *La désignation du lituus en hittite*, JCS 1, New Haven 1947, pp. 164-175.
——, *Eine hethitische Bronzestatuette und andere Funde aus Zara*, Anatolia/Anadolu 6, Ankara 1963, pp. 217-248.
——, *Istar auf dem Karahöyük*, Mélanges Mansel, ed. by E. Akurgal et al., II (TTKY VII:60a), Ankara 1974, pp. 703-707.
——, *Zylinder und Stempelsiegel aus Karahöyük bei Konya*, TTKY V:26, Ankara 1968.
BEHM-BLANCKE, M. R. & RITTIG, D., *Der Aslantaş von Eflâtun Pinar*, MDOG 102, Berlin 1970, pp. 89-99.
BERAN, T., *Hethitische Rollsiegel der Grossreichszeit*, IstMitt 8, Istanbul 1958, pp. 137-141; 9/10, Istanbul 1960, pp. 128-133.
——, *Die hethitische Glyptik von Bogazköy I*, Bogazköy-Hattusa V (WVDOG 76), Berlin 1967.
BITTEL, K., *Beitrag zu Eflâtun Pinar*, Bibliotheca Orientalis 10, Leiden 1953, pp. 2-5.
—— et al., *Bogazköy I-V*, Berlin 1935, 1938, 1957, 1969, 1975, especially III, pp. 25-31.
——, *Bogazköy, die Kleinfunde der Grabungen 1906-1912 I*, WVDOG 60, Leipzig 1937.
——, *Die Felsbilder von Yazilikaya*, Istanbuler Forschungen 5, Bamberg 1934.
——, *Hattusha: The Capital of the Hittites*, New York 1970, especially pp. 91-112.
—— et al., *Das hethitische Felsheiligtum Yazilikaya*, Berlin 1975.
——, *Eine hethitische Statuette aus Bogazköy*, Bulletin van de Vereniging tot Bevordering van de Kennis van de Antieke Beschaving 29, Leiden 1954, pp. 87-90.
——, *Les Hittites*, L'Univers des Formes, Paris 1976, pp. 51-233.
——, *Karabel*, MDOG 98, Berlin 1967, pp. 5-23.
——, *Eine kleinasiatische Nagelbronze*, Florilegium Anatolicum ... E. Laroche, Paris 1979, pp. 59-63.
——, *Die Reliefs am Karabel bei Nif ...*, AfO 13, Berlin 1941, pp. 181-193.
——, *Untersuchungen in Fraktin*, Archäologischer Anzeiger 54, Berlin 1939, pp. 566-568.
—— & NAUMANN, R., *Vorläufiger Bericht über die Ausgrabungen in Bogazköy 1938*, MDOG 77, Berlin 1939, pp. 1-46, especially pp. 24-28.
—— et al., *Yazilikaya*, WVDOG 61, Leipzig 1941.
BOEHMER, R. M., *Kleinasiatische Glyptik*, Propyläen Kunstgeschichte 14: Der alte Orient, ed. by W. Orthmann, Berlin 1975, pp. 437-453.
——, *Die Kleinfunde von Bogazköy*, Bogazköy-Hattusa VII, WVDOG 87, Berlin 1972.
——, *Die Kleinfunde aus der Unterstadt von Bogazköy*, Bogazköy-Hattusa X, Berlin 1979.
BÖRKER-KLÄHN, J., *Zur Lesung der Fraktin-Beischrift*, Oriens Antiquus 19, Rome 1980, pp. 37-48.
—— & BÖRKER, C., *Eflatun Pinar*, Jahrbuch des Deutschen Archäologischen Instituts 90, Berlin 1975, pp. 1-41.
BOSSERT, H. T., *Altanatolien*, Berlin, 1942.
BRANDENSTEIN, C. G. VON, *Hethitische Götter nach Bildbeschreibungen*, MVAeG 46, Leipzig 1942-43, no. 2.
CANBY, J. V., *Some Hittite Figurines in the Aegean*, Hesperia 38, Princeton 1969, pp. 141-149.
——, *Tesup Figurines and Anatolian Art of the Second Millennium B.C.*, Ph.D. dissertation, Bryn Mawr 1959.
DANMANVILLE, J., *Aperçus sur l'art hittite à propos de l'iconographie d'Istar-Sausga*, RHA 20, Paris 1962, no. 70, pp. 37-50.
——, *Iconographie d'Istar-Sausga en Anatolie ancienne*, RA 56, Paris 1962, pp. 9-30.
DARGA, M., *Über das Wesen des Huwasi-Steines ...*, RHA 84 (1969), pp. 5-24.
DEIGHTON, H. J., *The "Weather-God" in Hittite Anatolia*, BAR International Series 143, Oxford 1982.
DEMIRCIOGLU, H., *Der Gott auf dem Stier*, Berlin 1939.
DOGAN, S., *The Statuette of Ciftlik*, Anatolia/Anadolu 14 (1970), Ankara 1972, pp. 73-75.
DUSSAUD, R., *La Lydie et ses voisins aux hautes époques*, Babyloniaca 11, Paris 1929-30, pp. 69-174.
——, *Prélydiens, Hittites et Achéens*, Paris 1953.
EMRE, K., *Anatolian Lead Figurines and their Stone Moulds*, TTKY VI:14, Ankara 1971.
FRANKFORT, H., *Cylinder Seals*, London 1939, pp. 238-241, 284-288.
GOETZE, A., *Hittite Dress*, Corolla Linguistica: Festschrift F. Sommer, ed. by H. Krahe, Wiesbaden 1955, pp. 48-62.
——, *Hittite Myths, Epics, and Legends*, ANET³, Princeton 1969, pp. 120-128, 519.
——, *Hittite Rituals, Incantations, and Description of Festival*, ANET³, Princeton 1969, pp. 346-361.
——, *Kleinasien*, Handbuch der Altertumswissenschaft III.1.3.3.1, 2nd edition, Munich 1957, especially pp. 130-171: Die religiösen Anschauungen.
——, *The Priestly Dress of the Hittite King*, JCS 1, New Haven 1947, pp. 176-185.
GOLDMAN, H., *A Crystal Statuette from Tarsus*, Archaeologica Orientalia ... E. Herzfeld, Locust Valley 1952, pp. 129-133.
GÜTERBOCK, H. G., *Alte und neue hethitische Denkmäler*, In Memoriam Halil Edhem I, TTKY VII:5, Ankara 1947, pp. 59-70.
——, *Carchemish* (a review article), JNES 13, Chicago 1954, pp. 102-114, especially pp. 113-114.
——, *The God Suwaliyat Reconsidered*, RHA 19, Paris 1961, no. 68, pp. 1-18.

GÜTERBOCK, H. G., *Hethitische Götterbilder und Kultobjekte*, BAK, pp. 203-217.

——, *Das dritte Monument am Karabel*, IstMitt 17, Tübingen 1967, pp. 63-71.

——, *Hethitische Götterdarstellungen und Götternamen*, Belleten 7, Ankara 1943, pp. 295-317.

——, *Die Hieroglypheninschrift von Fraktin*, Festschrift L. Matous, ed. by B. Hruska, Budapest 1978, pp. 127-136.

——, *Les hiéroglyphes de Yazilikaya*, Paris, 1982.

——, *Hieroglyphische Miszellen*, Studia Mediterranea P. Meriggi ..., ed. by O. Carruba, Pavia 1979, pp. 235ff.

——, *Hittite Mythology*, Mythologies of the Ancient World, ed. by S. N. Kramer, Garden City 1961, pp. 139-179.

——, *Hittite Religion*, Forgotten Religions, ed. by V. Ferm, 1950.

——, *The Hurrian Element in the Hittite Empire*, Cahiers d'histoire mondiale 2, Paris 1954, pp. 383-394.

——, *Notes on Some Hittite Monuments*, AnatSt 6, London 1956, pp. 53-56.

——, *Religion und Kultus der Hethiter*, Historia Einzelschriften 7, Wiesbaden 1964, pp. 54ff.

——, Review of C. G. von Brandenstein, Hethitische Götter nach Bildbeschreibungen, Orientalia Nova Series 15, Rome 1946, pp. 482-496.

——, *Siegel aus Bogazköy I-II*, AfO Beihefte 5, 7, Berlin 1940, 1942.

——, *A Votive Sword with Old Assyrian Inscription*, Studies in Honor of B. Landsberger, ed. by H. G. Güterbock et al., Assyriological Studies 16, Chicago 1965, pp. 197-198.

——, *Yazilikaya*, MDOG 86, Berlin 1953, pp. 65-76.

——, *Yazilikaya: Apropos a New Interpretation*, JNES 34, Chicago 1975, pp. 273-277.

GURNEY, O. R., *Some Aspects of Hittite Religion*, Oxford 1977.

——, *The Hittites*, Penguin Books A 259, 2nd ed., Harmondsworth 1954, especially pp. 132-169: Religion.

HAAS, V., *Hethitische Berggötter und hurritische Steindämonen*, Berlin 1982.

—— & WÄFLER, M., *Yazilikaya und der Grosse Tempel*, Oriens Antiquus 13, Rome 1974, pp. 211-226.

HELCK, W., *Betrachtungen zur grossen Göttin und den ihr verbundenen Gottheiten*, Religion und Kultur der alten Mittelmeerwelt 2, Munich 1971.

HOGARTH, D. G., *Hittite Seals*, Oxford 1920.

JAKOB-ROST, L., *Zu den hethitischen Bildbeschreibungen*, MIO 8, Berlin 1963, pp. 161-217; 9, Berlin 1963, pp. 175-239.

KANTOR, H. J., *A Syro-Hittite Treasure in the Oriental Institute Museum*, JNES 16, Chicago 1957, pp. 145-162.

KARAMETE, K., *Idoles du Kültepe au Lycée et au Musée de Kayseri*, RHA 3, Paris 1934-36, no. 18, pp. 63-66; no. 24, 245-247.

KLENGEL, H., *Der Wettergott von Halab*, JCS 19, New Haven 1965, pp. 87-93, especially pp. 92-93.

LAROCHE, E., *Les dieux de Yazilikaya*, RHA 27, Paris 1969, pp. 61-109.

——, *Eflatun Pinar*, Anatolia/Anadolu 3, Ankara 1958, pp. 43-47.

——, *Koubaba, déesse anatolienne*, Eléments orientaux dans la religion grecque ancienne, Vendôme 1960, pp. 113-128.

——, *Le panthéon de Yazilikaya*, JCS 6, New Haven 1952, pp. 115-123.

——, *Recherches sur les noms des dieux hittites*, Paris 1947.

——, *Tessub, Hebat et leur cour*, JCS 2, New Haven 1948, pp. 113-136.

——, *Les dénominations des dieux antiques dans les textes hittites*, Anatolian Studies ... H. G. Güterbock, ed. by K. Bittel et al., Istanbul 1974, pp. 175-185.

LOUD, G., *The Megiddo Ivories*, OIP 52, Chicago 1939, pl. 11.

MACRIDY BEY, T., *La porte des sphinx à Euyuk*, MVAeG 13, Berlin 1908, no. 3.

MALTEN, L., *Der Stier in Kult und mythischem Bild*, Jahrbuch des Deutschen Archäologischen Instituts 43, Berlin 1928, pp. 90-139, especially pp. 107-114.

MAYER-OPIFICIUS, R., *Götterpaare in Kleinasien und Mesopotamien*, Studien zur Religion und Kultur Kleinasiens ... F. K. Dörner II, ed. by S. Şahin et al., Leiden 1978, pp. 595-601.

MELLAART, J., *The Late Bronze Age Monuments of Eflâtun Pinar and Fasillar*, AnatSt 12, London 1962, pp. 111-117.

MELLINK, M. J., *A Hittite Figurine from Nuzi*, Vorderasiatische Archäologie ... A. Moortgat, ed. by K. Bittel et al., Berlin 1964, pp. 155-164.

——, *Hittite Friezes and Gate Sculptures*, Anatolian Studies ... H. G. Güterbock, ed. by K. Bittel et al., Istanbul 1974, pp. 201-214.

——, *Observations on the Sculptures of Alaca Hüyük*, Anatolia/Anadolu 14 (1970), Ankara 1972, pp. 15-27.

MUSCARELLA, O. W., *Ancient Art: The Norbert Schimmel Collection*, Mainz 1974, nos. 123-125.

NAUMANN, R., *Einige Beobachtungen in Eflâtun Pinar*, Mélanges Mansel I, ed. by E. Akurgal et al., TTKY VII:60, Ankara 1974, pp. 467-474.

——, *Eine hethitische Statuette aus Kilikien*, Festschrift M. Wegner ..., ed. by D. Ahrens, Münster 1962, pp. 13-14.

NEVE, P., *Der grosse Tempel in Bogazköy-Hattusa*, Le temple et le culte, Compte rendu de la 20e Rencontre Assyriologique, Istanbul 1975, pp. 73-79.
——, *Eine hethitische Quellgrotte in Bogazköy*, IstMitt 19/20, Tübingen 1970, pp. 97-107.
——, *Hoftürme in den hethitischen Tempeln Hattusa's*, IstMitt 17, Tübingen 1967, pp. 78-92.
——, *Regenkult-Anlagen in Bogazköy-Hattusa*, IstMitt Beihefte 5, Tübingen 1961.
ÖZGÜÇ, N. *The Anatolian Group of Cylinder Seal Impressions from Kültepe*, TTKY V:22, Ankara 1965.
——, *Excavations at Acemhöyük*, Anatolia/Anadolu 10, Ankara 1968, pp. 1-52.
——, *Gods and Goddesses with Identical Attributes during the Period of Old Assyrian Trade Colonies*, Florilegium Anatolicum ... E. Laroche, Paris 1979, pp. 277-289.
——, *Ein hethitischer Stierkopf aus Tokat*, Anatolia/Anadolu 1, Ankara 1956, pp. 53-58.
——, *A Hittite Figurine Found at Dövlek*, TAD 5, Ankara 1949.
——, *Marble Idols and Statuettes from the Excavations at Kültepe*, Belleten 81, Ankara 1957, pp. 71-80.
——, *Seal Impressions from the Palaces at Acemhöyük*, Ancient Art in Seals, ed. by E. Porada, Princeton 1980, pp. 61-99.
——, *A Stamp Seal from Nigde Region and Four Seal Impressions Found in Acemhöyük*, Anatolia/Anadolu 15, Ankara 1971, pp. 17-26.
ÖZGÜÇ, T., *Ausgrabungen in Kültepe ... 1948 ...*, TTKY V:10, Ankara 1950.
ÖZGÜÇ, T& N., *Ausgrabungen in Kültepe ... 1949 ...*, TTKY V:12, Ankara 1953.
ÖZGÜÇ, T., *The Bitik Vase*, Anatolia/Anadolu 2, Ankara 1957, pp. 57-78.
——, *A Bronze Hittite Statuette*, Anatolian Studies ... H. G. Güterbock ..., ed. by K. Bittel et al., Istanbul 1974, pp. 253-255.
——, *A Bull-shaped Drinking Cup Discovered in the Vicinity of Kirşehir*, Mélanges Mansel II, ed. by E. Akurgal et al., TTKY VII:60a, Ankara 1974, pp. 963-965.
——, *A Figurine of a God from Anatolia in the Hermitage ...*, Florilegium Anatolicum ... E. Laroche, Paris 1979, pp. 291-296.
——, *Die Hethiter*, Museum für Anatolische Civilisationen, Ankara 1975.
——, *Kültepe-Kaniş ...*, TTKY V:19, Ankara 1959.
ORTHMANN, W., *Hethitische Götterbilder*, Vorderasiatische Archäologie ... A. Moortgat, ed. by K. Bittel et al., Berlin 1964, pp. 221-229.
——, *Hethitische Rundplastik, Hethitische Reliefkunst, Hethitisches Kunsthandwerk*, Propyläen Kunstgeschichte 14: Der alte Orient, ed. by W. Orthmann, Berlin 1975, pp. 419-437.
OSTEN, H. H. VON DER, *The Alishar Hüyük Seasons of 1930-1932 II*, OIP 29, Chicago 1937, pp. 1-286.
OTTEN, H., *Eine Beschwörung der Unterirdischen aus Bogazköy*, ZA 54, Berlin 1961, pp. 114-157, especially pp. 115, 148-149.
——, *Zur Datierung und Bedeutung des Felsheiligtums Yazilikaya*, ZA 58, Berlin 1967, pp. 222-240.
——, *Die Götter Nupatik ... von Yazilikaya*, Anatolia/Anadolu 4, Ankara 1959, pp. 27-37.
——, *Hethitische Totenrituale*, Berlin 1958.
——, *Neue Quellen zum Ausklang des Hethitischen Reiches*, MDOG 94, Berlin 1963, pp. 1-23, especially pp. 22-23.
——, *Die Religionen des alten Kleinasien*, Handbuch der Orientalistik, ed. by B. Spuler, vol. I.8.1.1, Leiden 1964, pp. 92-121.
——, *Ein Text zum Neujahrsfest aus Bogazköy*, OLZ 51, Berlin 1956, pp. 101-105.
POPKO, M., *Kultobjekte in der hethitischen Religion*, Warsaw 1978.
PUCHSTEIN, O. et al., *Boghaskoi, die Bauwerke*, WVDOG 19, Leipzig 1912.
RONZEVALLE, P. S., *Le cylindre Tyszkiewicz*, MUSJ 12, Beirut 1927, pp. 177-209; 15, Beirut 1930/31, pp. 261-280.
SCHAEFFER, C. F. A., LAROCHE, E. & GÜTERBOCK, H. G., *Matériaux pour l'étude des relations entre Ugarit et le Hatti*, Ugaritica III, Mission de Ras Shamra 8, ed. by C. F. A. Schaeffer, Paris 1956, pp. 1-163.
SCHULER, E. VON, *Kleinasien: Die Mythologie der Hethiter und Hurriter*, Wörterbuch der Mythologie, ed. by H. W. Haussig, Stuttgart 1965, pp. 141-215.
SEIDL, U., *Lapisreliefs und ihre Goldfassungen aus Karkamis*, IstMitt 22, Tübingen 1972, pp. 15-43.
STEINER, G., *Der Sukzessionsmythos in Hesiods Theogonie und ihren orientalischen Parallelen*, 1958.
TAŞYÜREK, O. A., *The Keben Hittite Rock Relief*, TAD 23, Ankara 1976, pp. 99-102.
UZUNOGLU, E., *Une figurine de fondation hittite*, Florilegium Anatolicum ... E. Laroche, Paris 1979, pp. 321-325.
VANEL, A., *L'iconographie du dieu de l'orage*, Paris 1965.
WEGNER, I., *Gestalt und Kult der Istar-Sawuska in Kleinasien*, Hurritologische Studien III, Alter Orient und Altes Testament 36, Kevelaer 1981.

INTRODUCTION

Colony Period (ca. 1925-1725 B.C.)

Two types of divine images are found in Anatolian houses at the end of the third millennium B.C.: alabaster 'idols'[1] and lead figurines, cast in stone molds which have been recovered from smelting shops or storerooms. The lead figurines were kept in the house; one was found on a kitchen floor. By the beginning of the second millennium, the stone 'idols' had gone out of fashion. The more naturalistic lead figurines, that in the late third millennium had been limited to images of the naked goddess supporting her breasts, remained popular and became more varied. Examples from the Karum Kanesh (Kültepe) IV-III period (ca. 2000-1925 B.C.; pl. Ia) display a triad consisting of the naked goddess supporting her breasts, her bearded consort and, between them, a daughter, naked like her mother, but holding on to her parents.[2] The father's pointed headdress, by comparison with later Anatolian images of the gods, confirms that this triad is divine and not human. In the earlier second millennium the gods' pointed caps are shown horizontally ridged on clay as well as on lead figurines. This may be a simplification of the multiple pairs of horns shown on Mesopotamian deities. We will show evidence below that a naked goddess usually accompanies the thunder god and apparently causes the rain to fall. Here, however, the only distinctive attribute of the god is a crescent pendant hanging from his double necklace. One wonders if it might indicate that he is the moon god. The pendant is absent from an otherwise almost identical lead triad excavated at Acemhöyük.[3] Only the position of the struts connecting the figures is slightly different on the Acemhöyük figurine.[4] On pl. Ia the details are somewhat clearer. We can see that the god's braids are looped around to the nape of his neck, and that his legs are shown in profile, with the border of his kilt running diagonally from left thigh to right waist. His left hand touches his wife's left shoulder; his right arm is to be thought reaching behind her right shoulder.

During the Karum Kanesh II-I or Assyrian Trading Colony period (ca. 1925-1725 B.C.) every house had its own protective deity; letters frequently mention 'your god, our god'. This evidence makes it plausible that the lead figurines represent the god or gods under whose protection the inhabitants had placed themselves.[5] Since their backs are flat, they must have been propped up and exposed frontally somewhere in the house. According to an interesting suggestion of Kutlu Emre's, a tiny grill found at Acemhöyük might represent a miniature altar. Some figurines were apparently cast in one piece with such a miniature altar, which could be folded into position by bending the soft lead (pl. IId).

---

[1] Nimet Özgüç in *Belleten* 81 (1957), pp. 71-80.

[2] *ALF*, pp. 131-133.

[3] *ALF*, pl. III: 3.

[4] At waist level the god is connected to the goddess by what is usually described as a strut. Representation of his phallus, however, would be quite in keeping with the explicit indication of sex on the female figures.

[5] *ALF*, p. 154.

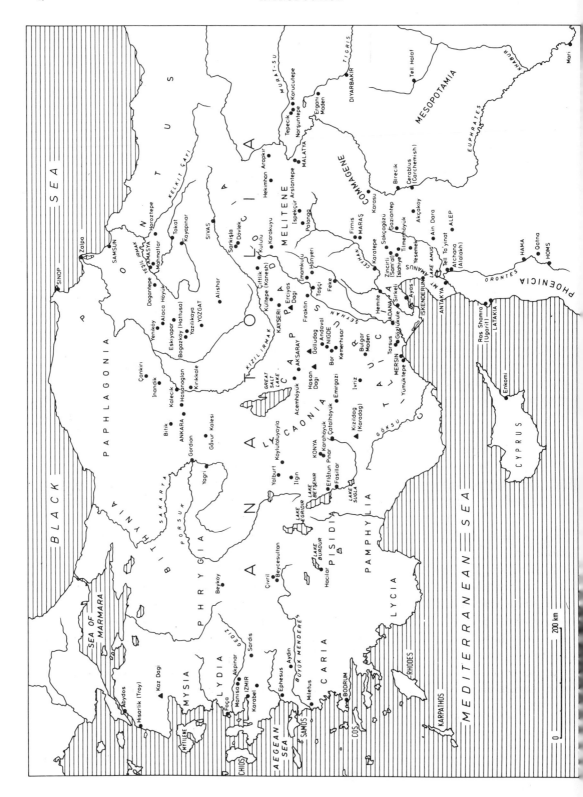

When one tries to identify iconographical types with deities mentioned in texts from the trading colonies, however, the evidence is often insufficient or contradictory. Even within one iconographical type conflicting versions may appear on contemporary monuments. The 'mistress of animals', probably an age-old deity native to Anatolia,[6] is shown seated on and peacefully surrounded by animals on Colony Period seals (pl. IXb-c), but standing, armed and lifting killed game on a figurine mold of the same period (pl. Id).

The master of animals or god of the chase, regularly shown bare-headed[7] and armed only with a crook on colony period seals (pl. VIIIb), appears with tall pointed cap and dagger on a mold from Kanesh.[8] The base for the figures on both of these molds is composed of two quadrupeds set head to head. In between is the pouring channel for the lead. On the figurine the soft lead quadrupeds could then be bent down and back to form a double-animal pedestal; other figurines were cast with a grill pedestal (cf. pl. IId). Although the large semicircular headgear relates her to the lead figurines of goddesses (pls. Ie, IIa, IIIa-b), the mistress of animals on the mold (pl. Id) represents a completely different style, more simplified even than that of the third-millennium molds. Her right hand has become a hook, from which a hare (?) hangs down, while her left hand is merged with a bird (?) she is holding up. Another bird seems attached to her left elbow. Falcon and hare are regularly held by the god of the chase on seals (pls. VIa, IXa). The other example we have included from the earlier half of the Assyrian Colony Period is the lead figurine of a goddess supporting her breasts (pl. Ie). While the gesture, suggesting a mother about to feed her child, is age-old and well represented among third-millennium figurines, the headgear is new. Although limited to a semicircle in the Colony Period, it is probably related to the full circle rendered three-dimensionally on seated goddesses of the Empire Period (pl. XLd). Since it is relatively flat, it looks like a large beret in side view (pl. IXc). Despite the three-dimensional rendering of breasts and navel, the lead goddess is apparently clothed. Hems are clearly visible on the shoulders, and pleats below the waist.

Lead figurines from the later half of the Colony Period display much greater variety. One type (pl. Ib), represented at Hattusa, the later Hittite capital, as well as at Kanesh, shows a bearded god shouldering a curved weapon. It seems to consist of a long, sinuous handle with a crescent-shaped blade, but without the fenestrations one sees on halberds of this period (cf. pl. IIa). It is probably a forerunner of the all-metal scimitar of the later second millennium B.C. The latter is shown on Empire Period reliefs in the hands of gods connected with war, hunting or death; apparently it was the knife with which a life was cut short. The lead god wears a wide belt with semicircular endings. Copper examples of these have been found. His dress has hatched borders on his left upper arm, down the front and along the bottom, suggesting he wore a kilt (sign of militance) and a wrap (token of dignity).

Alishar, another central Anatolian site with levels of the Colony Period, has yielded a mold from which lead figurines of a triad could be cast (pl. Ic). Here god, goddess and child all wear the same long dress. The god is armed with a short spear. Although the Syrian thunder god sometimes holds a spear with the point down (pl. Vc) and the spear

---

[6] See, e.g., the seated goddess flanked by leonine animals from Çatalhüyük in the preceding fascicle.
[7] Except on pl. IXa.
[8] *ALF*, pl. IV: 2.

stands for lightning on later Syrian reliefs,[9] there are too few links to lay this connection. Short spears are also carried by the Syrian god Amurru (?) who shoulders a gazelle-shaped crook on similar molds, not illustrated here.[10]

Kanesh itself has yielded another mold in the same style, but showing two daughters, one carried by the mother and one old enough to stand between her parents (pl. IIa). In addition to the short spear, the father shoulders an axe of which the blade is rendered by three parallel strokes; a fenestrated axe or halberd is probably intended. Although the connection with the thunder god remains tenuous, one is reminded of the later 'holy family' at Yazilikaya (pl. XXXI), which includes the thunder god's daughter and grand-daughter.

The lead figurine of a winged deity (pl. IIb) comes from Sam'al in the Syro-Anatolian border region. The large, rounded facial features and pronounced smile seem characteristic of Syria rather than Anatolia. The horizontally ridged cap, surmounted by a pompon, has the tips of two horns curving up in front. Kutlu Emre has drawn attention to the fact that the ringlets surrounding the face normally occur on females. Another possibly female feature is the vertically pleated bodice which envelops the torso, including the upper arms. In contradiction to this is the large, clearly indicated beard. One might think of a 'bearded lady' representing the bisexual deity of war and love (cf. p. XXIXc), were it not that a mold has been discovered at Kanesh displaying a bearded winged god (with prominent nipples) next to the goddess supporting her breasts.[11] The Sam'al figure's right hand holds a small vessel; the left fist is raised with the thumb on top in a gesture of greeting or blessing that we here see for the first time. Large, sickle-shaped wings emerge from the shoulders. One might mistake the prongs extending sideways and up-ward from the base for another pair of wings. From a drawing made shortly after its ex-cavation,[12] it is clear that the deity's skirt was complete at the time of finding, and the base had broken along an irregular line below the hem. Subsequently, the broken base was regularized by cutting away a low triangle. Originally, it must have looked like pl. IId, a mold of similar design that was found at Kanesh in a room containing crucibles, a blow pipe and 520 grams of lead. As explained above, the grill that was cast in one piece with the figurine may have been bent forward and its legs bent downward in order to form a pedestal that could also serve as a miniature altar. A third image of a winged, bearded deity is shown on pl. IIc. It does clearly have two more wings emerging from the base of its skirt. In addition, two birds fly up from its knees, while a third one is perched on its head. Here is another trait commonly associated with the goddess of love, both on roughly contemporary Syrian molds and seals and on later Anatolian reliefs.[13]

Another mold from Kanesh has a unique design in which a small god is shown in profile on a long-eared, hoofed animal behind the familiar breast-cupping goddess (pl. IIIa). Although one might be reminded of the later supreme goddess with her calf and her son at Yazilikaya (pl. XXXI), bovines are usually distinguished by clearly marked horns on

---

[9] See, e.g., the lightning god relief from Ugarit, Claude F. A. Schaeffer, *Ugaritica* II (Paris, 1949), pl. 23.
[10] *ALF*, pl. VI: 5, VII: 2.
[11] *ALF*, pl. VIII: 1.
[12] *ALF*, pl. VIII: 2a.
[13] E.g., Paolo Matthiae, *Ebla: Un impero ritrovato* (Turin, 1977), pls. 95, 99; *CANES I*, nos. 945-946, 968; Malatya relief: *Les Hittites*, fig. 278.

Colony Period seals (pls. Vc, VIb, VIIa-b), whereas the one hornless ungulate on these seals, with moderately long ears, carries a side-saddle or standing rider.[14] It therefore, more likely, represents a donkey or mule and may serve as a mount for the god (and goddess?) Pirwa.[15] Perhaps it is not too bold to connect the appearance of a donkey-riding god in the Colony Period, in Syria[16] as well as in Anatolia, with the importance of donkey-borne trade in those times.

Two lead figurines from Alishar show us a single goddess, one naked and broad-hipped, with hands cupping her breasts (pl. IIIb), the other clothed and slender, with hands placed at the waist, perhaps in an attitude of prayer (pl. IIIc).[17] A mold from Kanesh shows a naked goddess with conical headgear and spiral curls framing her face in an attitude that hints at the possible significance of many other naked goddesses (pl. IIId). She has removed her garment, the hems of which fall down from her spread hands, and displays her nudity. She is framed by two notched semicircles to which wings are attached below, while birds fly up by her hands (cf. pl. IIc). The scene is crowned by a winged sun (?) disk. One is forcibly reminded of contemporary Anatolian (pl. IXc) and slightly later Syrian seals[18] on which the consort of the thunder god unveils herself in or near the winged gate which may represent the rainbow, while rain fails from the sky. Many years ago Georges Contenau, in a monograph on the naked goddess in Mesopotamia, showed that she is actually labeled as Shala, the thunder god's wife, on some Old Babylonian seals.[19] In later Anatolian theology, her Hurrian and Hittite counterpart Salus was apparently paired with the grain god Kumarbi,[20] which makes sense if she called forth the rain. It will be noted that on pl. IIId the goddess herself has no wings.

Later iconography suggests that deities with wings represent major celestial bodies (cf. pl. XXIXa). Therefore the naked goddess from Karahöyük (pl. IVa) can hardly be other than the planet Venus that calls man to love at dusk or to war at dawn. In contrast to all the lead figurines we have seen thus far, this statuette presents bold curves both in outline and modeling, such as one also finds on Syrian seals toward 1750 B.C.[21] Her horns of divinity describe a double curve in the Mesopotamian tradition. The die caster has not eschewed the difficulty of foreshortening the base of the wings, so that they fit logically onto the goddesses' shoulders. By contrast the ivory naked goddess from Kanesh (pl. IVb) seems a clumsy work of art, in spite of its boldly three-dimensional treatment. She wears the turban or beret of the Anatolian goddesses (see discussion of pl. Id, above) and sup-

---

[14] *AG*, pls. XXVI: 77, I: 1.

[15] *AG*, pp. 67-69; Heinrich Otten in *JKF* 2 (1952/53), pp. 62-73; Emmanuel Laroche, *NDH*, p. 87.

[16] At Selenkahiye clay figurines of a god sitting side-saddle on a donkey occurred in Phase V, ca. 2000-1900, Maurits van Loon in *Le temple et le culte: Compte rendu de la 20e Rencontre Assyriologique Internationale* (Istanbul, 1975), pl. VI: 8.

[17] A clothed female with hands placed at the waist in what may be an attitude of prayer is another common type among clay figurines from Selenkahiye and elsewhere in Syria, *ibid.*, pl. VI: 7, left. She may be compared to the praying goddess so common on Mesopotamian seals of this period.

[18] *CANES* I, nos. 937-943, 967 and, especially, 944; Hans H. von der Osten, *Ancient Oriental Seals in the Collection of Mrs Agnes B. Brett* (OIP 37, Chicago, 1936), no. 90.

[19] Georges Contenau, *La déesse nue babylonienne* (Paris, 1914), pp. 114-118, figs. 14, 20, 21; for the later periods Contenau assumes a merger of several goddesses with Ishtar, p. 123. Shala's titles include ''lady of bright features'', ''of the dew'', ''irrigator'' and ''lady of the mountain,'' K. Tallqvist, *Akkadische Götterepitheta* (Studia Orientalia 7, Helsinki, 1938), p. 453.

[20] Emmanuel Laroche in *RHA* 35 (1977), p. 213.

[21] Edith Porada in Edith Porada, ed., *Ancient Art in Seals* (Princeton, 1980), p. 17.

ports her breasts, which seem small in proportion to the huge thighs. In part, the awkward effect is due to the difficulty of representing a seated figure frontally. The pubic triangle is made of other material, inlaid and painted red. That the statuette was made in a Syro-Anatolian milieu is suggested by its material (elephants existed in Syria at the time)[22] as well as by the greatly enlarged facial features and pronounced smile.

The casting of lead figurines from molds was a native Anatolian custom. As third-millennium examples from Troy, Izmir and Akhisar show,[23] it probably came to Central Anatolia from the west in Early Bronze Age III. The rolling of cylinder seals on clay, on the other hand, is a Mesopotamian custom that came along with the writing of clay tablets from the south and the east. Most of the sealed tablets have been found in the houses of Assyrian merchants in their *Karum* (colony) at Kanesh and it is not surprising that many of the seals they used came from Assyria, Babylonia or Syria, especially in the later half of the Colony Period.[24] Within this cosmopolitan assemblage of seal impressions a native Anatolian group can be distinguished on the basis of style (linear engraving, herringbone striations on garments and animals) and composition (figures surrounded by a wealth of associated motifs). It is best represented in the earlier half of the Colony Period (*ca.* 1925-1825 B.C.). In one archive of a native trader 60 out of 85 seal impressions belonged to this group, whereas in the archive of an Assyrian trader only 40 out of several hundreds had these native features.[25] The native roots of this cylinder seal group are also demonstrated by the occurrence of similar motifs on Colony Period stamp seals (pl. Xa-b). The stamp had been the native Anatolian sealing device and outlived the foreign cylinder seal, lasting into the first millennium B.C.

In spite of many distinctively native features it is hard to disentangle Anatolian from foreign elements even in the 'Anatolian' group of Colony Period seals. To a certain extent the seals may reflect the enrichment of Anatolian religion with Mesopotamian and Syrian elements that actually took place during the early second millennium. In the later second millennium Hittite iconography, while retaining many of the Mesopotamian-derived concepts, was to translate these into a distinctively Anatolian idiom. Nimet Özgüç has drawn attention to the fact that human worshippers, so common on contemporary Mesopotamian seals, are rare on Anatolian seals.[26] Such prominent Mesopotamian and Syro-Mesopotamian gods as the sun god with his saw stepping on his lion, Amurru, god of the western steppe on his gazelle and the lightning god stepping on his lion-eagle seem to pay homage to the seated war god on pl. Va, instead of being worshipped themselves. The recipient of homage on this seal is the one that seems to be the chief god of Kanesh, to judge by scenes like pls. IXb-c: he shoulders an axe and lifts a goblet, while his table is laden with flat bread. His seat is carried by a lion and a goat. As the bearded god with axe, lions and goats intervenes on the battlefield (P. VIIIa), Nimet Özgüç interprets him as the war god,[27] whose Hittite name may be Yarri.[28] On many Anatolian seals such

[22] Richard D. Barnett, *A Catalogue of the Nimrud Ivories* (London, 1957), pp. 164-166.

[23] *ALF*, pls. I: 1, I: 3, III: 1.

[24] Nimet Özgüç, *Seals and Seal Impressions of Level Ib from Karum Kanish* (TTKY V: 25, Ankara, 1968); *CANES I*, pp. 107-115.

[25] *AG*, p. 45.

[26] *AG*, p. 47.

[27] *AG*, p. 66.

[28] *Kleinasien*, p. 134, note 10.

Mesopotamian demigods as the bull-man holding a standard (pl. Va), the hero taming a lion (pls. Vb, VIa, VIIa-b, VIIIb) or the hero with flowing vase serve as terminal or filler (pls. Vb-c, IXb).

Just as the lion-tamer impersonates strength and courage, so the aquarius motif symbolizes abundance, especially of water, and seems particularly appropriate in the presence of the god of subterranean water on pl. Vb, of thunder, lightning and rain on pl. Vc, and also of the nature goddess on pl. IXb. The seated person on pl. Vb can be recognized as the water god Ea because his seat and feet are supported, as in Mesopotamia, by two goat-fish. Whereas the gods on pl. Va wear the expected pointed caps, with or without the horns of divinity, Ea wears the rounded fur (?) cap reserved for kings in Mesopotamia. The garment with fringes all over, on the other hand, is reserved for gods in Mesopotamia.[29] For this reason Nimet Özgüç is inclined to see gods even in those figures with flounced robes that seem to perform the duties of worshippers, such as those that lift their hands in prayer over fire altars and tables laden with joints of meat and pastry (pl. Vb). Her view is supported by pl. Vc, which shows a comparable figure with horned pointed cap. We yet have to discuss the most curious feature of this and many other seals from Kanesh and related sites, not only of the Anatolian group but also of the Old Assyrian, Provincial Babylonian and Syro-Cappadocian groups: it is the bull with a cone on its back (often crowned by a bird) that is the recipient of worship and must therefore stand for a god. We will see below that the various local thunder gods were often worshiped in the guise of a bull statue or statuette even in the later second millennium. That a statue is here intended appears clearly from pl. VIIb, where the bull stands on a pedestal supported by two bull-men and sticks out human hands to grasp the offerings set on the table. It might be tempting to see in the cone a symbol for Mount Erciyas (ancient Argaeus), the extinct volcano that towers above the plain of Kanesh, were it not that mountains are normally rendered by a scale pattern (cf. pl. XIIIc).

From later texts we know that many towns had their own thunder-and-lightning gods, also called storm or weather gods in modern translation. It is therefore not surprising to find more than one thunder-and-lightning god on the same seal (pls. Vc, IXa, IXc). I am calling 'lightning god' the one who is associated with lightning fork (pls. Va, Vc) and/or spear[30] (pls. Vc, VIa, IXa) or whip (pl. IXc). He often rides on the Mesopotamian lion-eagle (pls. Va, Vc),[31] and it is this feature especially that indicates his Syro-Mesopotamian origin. For this reason Nimet Özgüç calls him Adad, as opposed to his native Anatolian companion that I am calling 'thunder god.' The latter has a lower headgear and rides on a bull that he holds by a rein (pl. Vc, VIIIb, IXa, IXc). Occasionally he shoulders an axe (pl. VIIIb) that may, however, be carried by the lightning god as well (pls. VIa, VIIa). Note that the lightning god also often rides on a bull (pls. VIIa, IXa, IXc, Xa). The lightning god is the center of a mythological cycle of which we only get glimpses on earlier Mesopotamian and contemporary Syrian seals.[32] It involves the killing of a bull

---

[29] Rainer M. Boehmer in *RLA* 3 (1957-71), pp. 466-468.

[30] See note 9.

[31] Also called lion-griffin; he has an eagle's tail and eagle's wings, carved as parallel diagonal or curving strokes.

[32] Henri Frankfort, *Cylinder Seals* (London, 1939), pp. 124-129, 269-271. For a partly different interpretation, see Elizabeth Williams-Forte in L. Gorelick & E. Williams-Forte, eds., *Ancient Seals and the Bible* (Malibu 1983), pp. 24-30.

(pl. VIb)[33] and/or the disrobing of the god's consort (pls. Vc, VIb, IXc),[34] which causes the rain to fall, either from the lion-eagle's lowered head (pls. Va, Vc)[35] or, in parallel strokes, from the sky onto the earth, represented by a rectangle (pls. VIIa, IXa, IXc, Xa).[36] The locale of this scene is the winged gate (undoubtedly representing the rainbow),[37] always shown in side view on Anatolian seals as a gatepost with attached wing and ropes (pls. VIa, VIIa, IXa, IXc). On pl. Xa it continues over the scene as an arc from which rain falls onto the rectangular earth (note that the earth is represented by a rectangle with crossbars on the later relief of pl. XXVIIb). On pl. VIa the gate exceptionally rests on the back of a goat-fish, the animal of the water god, and the lightning spear is left hanging from the gate's wing (this may also be the case on pl. IXa). The wing's feathers are carved as parallel diagonal curves.

On pl. Vc the recipient of worship rests his feet on a lion that seems to have eaten a goat; its head is left over. Since lion and goat are the animals of the war god and since he is often the goal of a divine procession, Nimet Özgüç is undoubtedly right in considering him the war god.[38] The sun-and-moon emblem—as she has also shown—is prominent on many other seals that demonstrably show non-astral deities; in divine processions it floats in front of the thunder god and even appears on his horned rounded cap (pls. VIa, IXc).

The third god that appears on pl. VIa is the god of the chase, recognizable by the crook over his shoulder, the falcon on his hand and the hare he carries. He is usually shown in a hornless rounded cap (pls. VIa, VIIIb), but on pl. IXa he wears a horned pointed cap. His identity there is proven by the stag that serves as his mount. On seals not shown here, the god with crook, falcon and rounded cap rides on a stag.[39] He corresponds to the later description of a god who protects the fields (see below) and is probably to be thought as a nature god who, if favorably disposed, will provide the hunter with game.

The possible significance of breast-cupping goddess and bull-stabbing god on pl. VIb has been discussed above. It is doubtful whether the five large dots could in this case stand for the rain which usually accompanies such scenes. The appearance of the water god Ea with his two-faced vizier Usmu is certainly appropriate in this context. Ea has water emanating from his shoulders and forming a wavy arch over him.

Plate VIIa is important because it clearly shows an enigmatic cult object regularly used in the Colony Period. In the main scene, below the pitcher from which the worshipper is filling the god's beaker, we see a small globular jar such as held by the hero with flowing vase and other water-dispensing deities and, left of this, a tube with a rounded protuberance halfway down. Nimet Özgüç has called it the elixer vase, because it is sometimes physically connected to the globular jar.[40] It has been suggested that it may have been a pipette with which liquid was transferred from a larger to a smaller vessel.[41]

---

[33] Cf. Frankfort, *op. cit.*, pl. XXIIe, a Mesopotamian seal of *ca.* 2250 B.C.
[34] Cf. Frankfort, *op. cit.*, pl. XLIVd, Text fig. 86, Syrian seals of *ca.* 1600 B.C.
[35] Cf. Frankfurt, *op. cit.*, pl. XXIIa, a Mesopotamian seal of *ca.* 2250 B.C.
[36] For various other renderings of rain in this context, see Frankfort, *op. cit.*, pls. XXIIa, e, XLIV i.
[37] Shown as an arched guilloche or water motif on *CANES* I, no.,944 E.
[38] *AG*, p. 76.
[39] *AG*, pls. XXI: 64, XXIII: 69.
[40] *AG*, pls. VIII: 22, IX: 26, XX: 59.
[41] Edith Porada, *Mesopotamian Art in Cylinder Seals of the Pierpont Morgan Library* (New York, 1947), p. 34 suggested the jar is a measuring vessel and the "tube" a rod with a measuring line wound around it—appropriate symbols for the god of sun and justice.

It must have been made of perishable material, as excavations have failed to produce such objects to date. On pl. VIIb we see another characteristic vessel, of which pottery examples have been found in Karum Kanesh level II (*ca.* 1925-1825): the two-handled beer jar; two drinking reeds have been stuck into it.

Plate VIIIa shows us the war god shouldering an axe and surrounded by lion and goats, on the location of his main activities: the battle field. In the upper register a kneeling archer is surrounded by headless corpses; in the lower, a spearman is about to kill a victim. In his left hand he carries the severed head of another victim. Although not marked as a god, the spearman might be compared to the description of a second war god (see discussion of pl. XXVIIIa). Animal heads may be left over from the lion's victims; vultures are feeding on human and animal remains. Obviously violent death in one form or the other is the god's concern. The hunting god is often shown kneeling, as on pl. VIIIb. Among the various types of animals that illustrate his mastery of nature are crab, lizard and bearded sphinx.

Plates IXb and IXc seem to show the chief deities of central Anatolia in the Colony Period. While the war god, here seated and receiving libations, has been mentioned before, we now see that his consort is even more elaborately treated. Her seat—in the shape of a goat on pl. IXc—rests on two leonine creatures. These elements together apparently make up her statue, because on pl. IXc they in turn rest on a pedestal supported by two human-headed bulls. A closely related seal shows a third register underneath, consisting of a rectangle (the earth?) flanked by lambs.[42] A lamb is perched on her hand in pl. IXb. Among the panoply of animals surrounding her on pl. IXc are many birds, a tree and a female (?) sphinx. Birds seem perched on her beret in pls. IXb and IXc (?). On account of her lion throne, especially, one is reminded of the age-old Anatolian goddess seated between two leonine creatures, who was worshipped into Roman times as Cybele.[43] Sheep were offered to Kubabat at Kanesh in the Colony Period.[44] Beside the pitchers, beakers and beer jar, two types of altars are seen on pls. IXb-c: 'fruit stands', of which pottery examples have been found, carrying flat bread and buns, and probably foldable wooden or basketry tables, on which doughnuts and poultry are visible.

Two stamp seal impressions of the later Colony Period from Acemhöyük are shown on pl. Xa-b. The first has been mentioned above in discussing lightning god and winged gate. Plate Xb is unique in showing an obelisk-like column as object of worship. Its conic finial might be compared to the cone on the bull (pls. Vb, VIIb). In contemporary Syria obelisks occasionally occur in temple precincts,[45] but do not themselves seem to be objects of worship. From the later second millennium, however, there is ample textual evidence for standing stones serving as divine images (see below). Here the seated lady holding a plant may represent the goddess herself. Two bulls' heads are attached to the obelisk and a third one, detached, is seen above.

---

[42] *AG*, p. 27, fig. 6.
[43] Emmanuel Laroche in *Elements orientaux dans la religion grecque ancienne* (Vendôme, 1960), pp. 113-128.
[44] Hans Hirsch, *Untersuchungen zur altassyrischen Religion* (AFO Beiheft 13/14, Graz, 1961), pp. 27-28. The Anatolian deities most often mentioned in the Old Assyrian merchants' letters are the god Ana (13 ×) and the goddess Kubabat (4 ×).
[45] Maurice Dunand, *Fouilles de Byblos* II, pp. 644-652, 878, pls. 21-32.

Fig. 1. Impression of seal from Aydin, 1700-1600. After L. Delaporte, *Catalogue des cylindres orientaux II* (Musée du Louvre), p. 195, no. A 927.

Old Hittite Period (ca. 1700-1400 B.C.).

Few objects dating from this period have a bearing on iconography. Plate Xd shows what is probably a foundation figurine, if one may compare him with earlier Mesopotamian figurines of kings ending in pegs and much earlier ones of deities similarly terminated below.[46] The idea was to nail to the earth, with divine protection, the building one was about to build. About his identity we can tell no more than that he belongs to the young, militant type of god, with bare chest and wide belt, that was best suited to protect a building against evildoers (cf. pl. XXIV).

The statuette from Dövlek (pl. Xc) can be more readily identified because of his posture, which is that of a whole series of Syrian bronzes showing a smiting god.[47] 'The smiter' is a possible etymology for both the Syrian name, Reshef, and the Hurrian name, Tesub, of the lightning god. Occasionally the spear that he wields is preserved on the bronzes; it is regularly shown on reliefs and seals (pl. XIa). That it represents the lightning is sometimes made clear by flames issuing from it.[48] On pl. XIa he is smiting an enemy, who is then cremated by mourners. The corpse has a conical cap, such as found (made of gold or silver) in graves at Kanesh.[49] Below the bier is food (symbolized by bull's head and sheep's head) and drink (symbolized by a jar) for the life hereafter. Next comes a downpour that I would connect to the disrobing goddess on the left. The water, with a swimmer in it, continues into the subterranean domain of the water god, where it is

---

[46] Subhi A. Rashid in *RLA* 3 (1957-71), pp. 655-661; Richard S. Ellis, *Foundation Deposits in Ancient Mesopotamia*, New Haven, 1968.

[47] Dominique Collon in *Levant* 4 (1972), pp. 111-134; Ora Negbi, *Canaanite Gods in Metal* (Tel Aviv, 1976), pp. 29-41; Helga Seeden, *The Standing Armed Figurines of the Levant* (Prähistorische Bronzefunde I: 1), Münich, 1980.

[48] See note 9.

[49] Tahsin Özgüç in *Belleten* 19 (1955), pp. 71-72. Evidence of cremation on a wooden bier was also found at Kanesh, Tahsin Özgüç, *1948 Ausgrabungen in Kültepe* (TTKY V:10, Ankara, 1950), pp. 163-164.

caught in a variety of vessels. Above, the water god drinks from a bowl filled by his two-faced vizier, who introduces three gods. They hold three crooks down, while Ea holds a double axe and three crooks (or is it a scourge?) up.[50] The bordering twists and spirals also clearly signify water. A seal in the Louvre with a closely comparable scene is said to come from Aydin in southwest Anatolia (fig. 1).[51] The double-axe motif, too, points in that direction. This divine weapon remained popular in first-millennium Caria.[52]

The slightly later five-faceted seal (pl. XIb) comes from southeast Anatolia. For the first time the gods appear in pointed cap with one horn only, seen in profile. At least one of the seated figures wearing a tall pointed headgear, namely the one holding up a small goat as in pl. IXb, must be female. The other goddesses' beret, being veiled, takes the outline of a cylinder, rising somewhat in front. The signs "lightning," "well-being" (a triangle) and "life" (a bowknot) are strewn in the upper field. The asymmetric altar can be compared to those on pl. XVIIa; the gesture of libating into the ground is also paralleled there. We recognize a few deities we have seen before, such as the hunting god (cf. pl. VIIIb, IXa) and the mistress of animals (cf. pl. IXb). On the adjoining facet she may be shown again, this time as the mistress of plants; she is attended by an eagle-headed genius and a goat supports her seat, as on a Colony Period seal.[53] One might also compare her to the description of Iyaya (see below).

From Bitik near Ankara we have a fragmentary example of a relief vase picturing a probably religious feast (pl. XIIa); a complete example found at Inandik has not yet been published. The lowest preserved register of the Bitik vase shows two men with weapons, apparently ready to attack each other in what may be a sporting event that was part of the feast; in the middle register men are carrying food and drink to the scene of festivities, which is visible in the top register. There a large, long-dressed figure is standing in front of a building with a portico; Kurt Bittel interprets her tentatively as the goddess in front of her temple.[54] Through the portico we glimpse an event taking place inside: a seated man whose body is enveloped in a long cloak offers drink to a seated woman whose veil he is lifting. The public part of a wedding probably culminated in removal of the bridal veil in ancient western Asia.[55]

Ritual texts of the Empire Period (see below) provide ample evidence for drinking and libating out of animal-shaped vessels. In rituals for the thunder god these vessels took the shape of bulls and in some instances such vessels might even serve as the cult statue or

---

[50] For partly different interpretations, see P. S. Ronzevalle in *MUSJ* 12 (1927), pp. 177-209, 15 (1930/31), pp. 261-280; Henri Frankfort, *Cylinder Seals* (London, 1939), pp. 247, 285-288; René Dussaud, *Prélydiens, Hittites et Achéens* (Paris, 1958), pp. 89-101; Rainer M. Boehmer in *Der alte Orient*, p. 446; R. L. Alexander in *Anatolica* 5 (1973-76), pp. 141-215.

[51] Louis Delaporte, *Catalogue des cylindres orientaux II* (Musée du Louvre, Paris, 1923), no. A 927 on p. 195, pl. 96; cf. same, *Catalogue des cylindres orientaux ... de la Bibliothèque Nationale* (Paris, 1910) no. 425, an Old Syrian seal. It is almost as if several seal-cutters had copied the same example available, perhaps, in a wall-painting.

[52] A. Dumont in *Bulletin de correspondance hellénique* 3 (1879), pp. 129-130; R. Ganszyniec in *Paulys Real-Encyclopädie ...* 23 (Stuttgart, 1924), cols. 277-282 and 286-307.

[53] *AG*, p. 27, fig. 6. A 17th-century seal from Nigde, published by Nimet Özgüç in *Anadolu* 15 (1971), pp. 17-26, shows a god with trident, a goddess with plants and a goddess facing an eagle genius over a wild sheep's head.

[54] *Les Hittites*, p. 144.

[55] The elusive evidence on the institution of the sacred marriage has been reviewed by J. Renger and J. S. Cooper in *RLA* 4 (1972-75), pp. 251-269.

focus of worship itself. The magnificent examples unearthed in the Hittite capital (pl. XIIb) are about one-quarter life-size and have a funnel-shaped opening on the withers and ropes connected to a nose ring in painted relief. This feature is a clear link to the iconography of the thunder god (cf., e.g., pl. IXa).

There is some evidence in Anatolia for the use of bull masks in the cult—no doubt of the thunder god—as in later second-millennium and early first-millennium Cyprus.[56] On plate XIIIa we see a human figure, enveloped in a cloak such as worn by priests, kings and women, playing the tambourine. Although the mask is not clearly terminated and one might therefore argue that we here have a bull-headed genius, the later association of masks with music in Mesopotamia makes the use of a mask here more likely.[57] On pl. XLIIa we will see a clearly masked personage flanked by figures with tall crowns and crooks.

On another cult scene (pl. XIIIb) we see a young man whose kilt has an extension covering the back leg (cf. pl. XIIa) offering up a calf's head which is probably one of the many rhyta described in cult inventories as a 'bull's (head and) neck' (see below).

Pierre Amiet has dated pl. XIIIc to the 15th century B.C. by comparing the human-head border on north Syro-Mesopotamian seals of this date.[58] If the goats' and stags' heads below refer to the hunt of the lower register, the men's heads must have fallen during the battle of the gods of which we see the outcome in the upper register. The lightning god is shown brandishing his double whip, with one leg on a chariot drawn by two bulls. The griffin behind him could be a reminiscence of his lion-eagle (cf. pl. Va, c). His consort, facing him, has removed her garment. The ends of her belt hang down as on pl. IIId. Streams of water emanate from her shoulders. The couple's victory is celebrated on the left by the same triad we saw on pl. XIa. Here the moon god goes in front, holding a beaker, the thunder god in the middle, a horn in his hand, star and crescent in the sky, and the sun god holding a saw goes behind, flames issuing forth from his body. After him comes the goddess of war and love (cf. pl. XXIXc). She also holds a beaker and her sandals are looped, like those of the naked goddess (cf. pl. XLb). On the right the couple's victory is acknowledged by various chthonic deities: first a libation is poured from a beaked pitcher by an eagle genius, envoy of the earth and nature goddess (cf. pl. XIb). Then a snake-haired human figure emerges naked from beneath a deified pile of rocks; surely this is Ullikummi of the well-known Hurrian myth.[59] The latter is followed by a mountain god with only the lower part of his body formed by scaly rocks (cf. pl. XXVI). Both mountain gods raise their fists together as if ready to fight (or shackled? cf. pls. XXVIb, XXX). In the lower register the hunting god, with bow and spear, this time mounted on a lion, confronts four lions; his falcon sits on a tree. A lion seems to lead four chariots with human stag hunters that follow behind. The literary associations of the upper register clearly lead us to the Hurrian-speaking southeast of Anatolia; it is even further

[56] Jacques C. Courtois in Claude F. A. Schaeffer, ed., *Alasia* I (Mission Archéologique d'Alasia 4, Paris, 1971), pp. 151 ff., especially fig. 2 and pp. 226-231, 240-253; Vassis Karageorghis, *Kition* (London, 1976), pp. 102-105, pls. 79-82.

[57] Richard D. Barnett & Margarete Falkner, *The Sculptures of ... Tiglath-Pileser* (London, 1962), pls. I-II: men clapping hands and wearing lion mask to celebrate victory.

[58] Pierre Amiet, *Bas reliefs imaginaires de l'Ancien Orient* (Hotel de la Monnaie exhibition catalog, Paris, 1973), p. 135: no. 390.

[59] Hans G. Güterbock in *MAW*, pp. 164-172; Albrecht Goetze in *ANET³*, pp. 121-125.

[60] Edith Porada, *Ancient Iran* (London, 1965)/*The Art of Ancient Iran* (New York, 1965), pp. 96-102; Machteld J. Mellink in *Iranica Antiqua* 6 (1966), pp. 72-87.

east, in west Iran around 1000 B.C., that we find the closest iconographical correspondence on the gold beaker from Hasanlu.[60] There we see the same triad of gods, the disrobing goddess, the bull chariot and the thunder god fighting with the semi-human rock pile resting on snakes.

Empire Period (ca. 1400-1185 B.C.)

In the Empire Period the citadel at Alaca Höyük, northeast of the capital, was protected by an inner city wall with a monumental gateway, the jambs of which were sculptured on the outside with massive female sphinxes in high relief (pl. XIV). The Egyptian concept of combining the images of king or queen and lion into a sphinx had influenced Syria and Anatolia since the early second millennium (see pl. IXc), and the hairstyle of these female sphinxes also goes back to Egyptian examples. But the significance of the Syro-Anatolian sphinx certainly differed from that of its Egyptian prototype: here the semi-divine creatures have the double function of welcoming well-doers and frightening off, with their lions' paws, any possible evil-doers. On the andesite slabs which line the outside substructure of the gate the arriving visitor is told what purpose the buildings inside mainly serve: the cult of the thunder god on the left and that of his consort on the right. Within the gateway the left and right-hand jamb must have shown the divine couple's daughter and granddaughter in low relief, entering the precinct on a double eagle that has caught two hares (pl. XVa, cf. pl. XXXI). At the tail end of the procession from the left are three beardless men raising their right fist in adoration (pl. XVb). Their cloaks reach down to the calves and beneath them one can see the tails of their cutaway-like kilts (cf. pls. XIIa, XIIIb). That they are priests is evident from the next slab, on which one of them leads animals to sacrifice (pl. XVc). Finally, queen and king confront a bull statue over a wickerwork altar (pl. XVd).[61] The queen apparently wore a tall headgear with a veil over it falling down her back (cf. pl. XVIIa). She has a small ring in her ear and lifts her right fist in greeting or prayer. With her left hand she gathers the loose garment below her right elbow against the body; it falls down in parallel curving pleats. In ritual acts one had to be particularly careful not to knock any cult objects over with loose clothing. For similar reasons the king always wears a cloak enveloping even his right elbow. It reaches down to the tips of his boots. Otherwise, it is undistinguishable from the priests' cloak. Priests and king wear large earrings and round caps, but the king's cap has a double border (cf. pl. XXXIV). The sculptor apparently started to work on the crook from both ends and had some difficulty in making them meet. Curving copper caps for such royal insignia were found in the rich third-millennium tombs at Alaca Höyük.[62] The bull that is being adored might be taken for an adjunct of the storm god; cult inventories, however, prove that this god himself was often worshiped in the guise of a bull or even, at times, of a bull-shaped vessel (see below). The symmetry with the scene at the right (pl. XVIc) suggests that such is the case here too. The bull, set on a tall pedestal decorated with niches, is seen in side view but with frontally shown horns, as on Old Anatolian seals (cf. pls. Vc,

---

[61] The diagonal hatching suggests wickerwork. Note, however, that a stone altar inscribed by Tudhaliya IV was found at Emirgazi, I. J. Gelb, *Hittite Hieroglyphic Monuments* (OIP 45, Chicago, 1939), p. 14; B. Hrozny, *Les inscriptions hittites hiéroglyphiques* I: 3 (Praque, 1937), pl. 78 (our pl. XVIIb).
[62] Hamit Z. Kosay, *Les fouilles d'Alaca Höyük ... 1937-1939* (TTKY V:5, Ankara, 1951), pl. 180.

VIb, VIIa-b). Cheek muscles, mane and dewlap are rendered by shallow relief strips. Shoulder blade, pectoral and thigh muscles are stylized into shield, walking-stick and tulip patterns which recur on the seal of king Muwattali (*ca.* 1300).[63] On account of this very specific resemblance, and of the important part also played by a bull on the king's seal, one might perhaps attribute the Alaca Höyük sculptures to his reign. Kurt Bittel has drawn attention to features linking them to Old Hittite works and differing from 13th-century art.[64] Moving to the left from the left edge of pl. XVb, more temple personnel comes to assist at a second bull worship scene: acrobats, a sword eater (pl. XVIb) and musicians (pl. XVIa). One of the acrobats, a mere boy, his head shaven Egyptian-style but for a lock, climbs a free-standing ladder while the other is ready to catch him. Both he and the sword-eater have short locks curling up from the front of their caps. The front musician plays a lute with long streamers. Behind him a young man holds a short-necked, curly-tailed animal on a leash (?); as monkeys are a standard element in ancient Near Eastern scenes of merriment,[65] a monkey may be intended here.[66] More figures on the side of the first bull statue block (visible in pl. XIVb) included a priest holding a kind of halberd (or is it a pipette? cf. pl. VIIa). On pl. XVIc all three priests are carrying such halberds toward a seated goddess who is dressed like the queen on pl. XVd; in addition she wears a triple necklace and holds a large three-petaled flower (or bursting pomegranate?) in her left while she drinks from a bowl in her right hand. At a door of the building the lightning god was shown in human form, drinking from a bowl while a priest worships him with both fists lifted, thumbs on top (pl. XVId).[67] The god wears a pointed cap with four horns down the front. His hair ends in a pigtail at waist level. The god's mace, visible behind his hair, must be clasped by his left upper arm while his left hand comes around to support the right elbow, like the queen's on pl. XVd. Faint traces suggest the mace handle was first shown across the right shoulder. The god's plaid-covered throne rests on a podium with three horns (?) down the front.

    Although rock outcrops—especially if connected to a spring—were revered from early times, and rock reliefs had been carved in Mesopotamia and Iran since the third millennium, the Hittite rock reliefs that left such a lasting mark upon Anatolia may all date to the 13th century B.C.[68] We first show one of the rock reliefs that bears the name of the great king Hattusili III (*ca.* 1275-1250, pl. XVIIa). A puzzling feature of this relief is the assimilation in dress of king and queen (so marked by their names) to god and goddess. The king even wears the horn of divinity on his pointed cap while, as Robert L. Alexander has discovered,[69] the queen wears the Hittite sun symbol or *signe royal* on her tiara (perhaps a veiled, halo-like beret as on pl. XLd, seen in side view). One wonders if the relief was carved after the king's death (cf. pl. XXXIV), or even after the death of both

---

[63] Hans G. Güterbock. *Siegel aus Bogazköy II* (AfO Beiheft 7, Berlin, 1942), pp. 50-51.

[64] *Les Hittites*, pp. 200-201.

[65] E.g., drummers with monkey on vase from Tello, Iraq: André Parrot, *Sumer* (Paris, 1960), fig. 286; man with flute-playing monkeys on clay plaque from Ur, Ruth Opificius, *Das altbabylonische Terrakottarelief* (Berlin, 1961), no. 630.

[66] Bittel, *Les Hittites*, p. 194, thinks of an animal-shaped vessel. Animal-shaped musical instruments also occur frequently in earlier Mesopotamian scenes.

[67] Hans G. Güterbock, *Guide to the Hittite Museum in the Bedesten at Ankara* (Istanbul, 1946), p. 57.

[68] Bittel, *Les Hittites*, p. 171.

[69] *JNES* 36 (1977), pp. 199-207.

king and queen.[70] If not, this is the only example from Empire times of Hittite royalty donning divine garb in their desire to identify themselves with their respective deities.[71] To judge by the crook over his shoulder the male deity is the hunting god. Both deities seem to proffer the sign 'well-being' (a triangle) on their left fist. Higher up are the logograms for their names.[72] In front of them stand asymmetric wickerwork altars with tablecloths hanging down toward them. King and queen libate onto the ground. The seated goddess holds a drinking bowl up in her right hand. In contrast to the queen, whose facial features at least are superficially engraved, the figure of the goddess seems to have been blocked out but left unfinished. A falcon, also belonging to the hunting god's entourage, is perched on her altar. Plate XLb shows she is the hunting god's mother. A falcon is also later the symbol of Kubaba, strongly suggesting some link between that popular goddess of the first millennium and the hunting god's mother of the second millennium. Although diagonally hatched and therefore probably not rendering stone, the altars are not unlike the stone altar from Emirgazi (pl. XVIIb).[73] On another rock relief in the Taurus mountains (pl. XVIIc) we see, on the left, a prince shouldering his bow and walking with a tall stick in front of him. Facing away from him, so perhaps leading him, the thunder god rides on his bull-drawn chariot over the backs of three mountain gods with bent caps and raised fists (cf. pl. XXX), each supported by an eagle-headed genius. On the right his consort appears (cf. pls. IXc, XIIIc), removing her garment and standing on a lion-eagle with four pairs of wings.[74] The figure in horned pointed cap on pl. XVIIIa, shouldering a bow and walking with a tall stick in front of him, looks like a god at first sight. If we combine the evidence from pls. XVIIa and c, however, we may possibly see in him a local king of this far western region of Anatolia.[75] Another rock relief located close to the Aegean is shown on pl. XVIIIb. Weathered almost beyond recognition, but still impressive on account of its dimensions, it appears to represent the age-old Anatolian mother goddess that became Matar Kubileja for the Phrygians, Kuvav for the Lydians and Cybele for the Greeks.[75a] The monument overlooks a spring-fed pond at the foot of the slope. To judge by the identical inscriptions, it was carved at the order of the same prince as pictured at Imamkulu, 750 km to the east (pl. XVIIc).[76]

The part masonry, part rock-cut hilltop monument illustrated on pl. XIXa contained a corbeled chamber, now empty. Part masonry hilltop monuments are found inside the

---

[70] Robert L. Alexander does not seem to exclude this possibility, *loc. cit.*, note 23.

[71] In the earlier first millennium B.C. we shall encounter instances of this desire in the reliefs at Malatya, see following fascicle, pl. IIa.

[72] Hans G. Güterbock in B. Hruška et al., eds., *Festschrift Lubor Matouš* (Budapest, 1978), pp. 127-136. Strangely enough, the left-hand figure seems to be simply labeled "the god". Puduhepa is described as "Puduhepa, great queen, daughter of the land Cilicia, beloved of the god." The goddess seems to be labeled "goddess Hi", which is generally interpreted as short for Hebat.

[73] See note 61.

[74] Hans G. Güterbock in Onofrio Carruba, ed., *Studia Mediterranea Piero Meriggi dicata* (Pavia, 1979), pp. 237-238. The photograph on p. 243 clearly shows that the supporting genii have eagles' heads.

[75] Kurt Bittel in *MDOG* 98 (1967), pp. 5-23; Hans G. Güterbock in *IstMitt* 17 (1967), pp. 63-71. The inscription probably reads "King X, son of King Y" and the name of King Y seems to recur on another rock inscription nearby.

[75a] Two scholars have recently proposed that the relief on Mount Sipylos represents not the mother goddess but a stooping mountain god (cf. pl. XVIIc etc.), Peter Z. Spanos in *BAK*, pp. 477-483, and Kay Kohlmeyer in *Acta Praehistorica et Archaeologica* 15 (1983), pp. 28-34.

[76] See note 74 and Helmut T. Bossert in *Orientalia N.S.* 23 (1954), pp. 139, 144-147.

Hittite capital as well and correspond to the description of certain royal mausolea. The rock wall of the terrace has been smoothed and carved with the figures of a bearded god with four horns down the front of his cap and a beardless god, both greeting a seated deity that lifts a drinking bowl and is only blocked out and apparently unfinished.

Stelae with divine images in relief became common in the Syro-Anatolian border region in the first millennium B.C. Plate XIXb, is so close to Hittite Empire reliefs in style that we treat it here. The inscription says 'storm god of lightning' and he must have held a spear with its point down. His left fist proffers the sign 'well-being' as on pl. XVIIa. Unusual are the tassels that hang down from scabbard and kilt. Stelae with or without images are often mentioned as the focus of worship in cult inventories and, where old and new cult objects are contrasted, stelae are among the older. Plate XIXc seems to show a prince worshiping twin stelae placed upon a wattle-and-daub pedestal. This statue or stela base was found near the main temple in the Hittite capital, which in its extant form dates from about 1275-1250 B.C. The relief block may well derive from a predecessor building.

In Anatolia, as in Mesopotamia, temples had important economic as well as religious functions. In the Hittite capital the main temple, at least, was surrounded by extensive storerooms; priests and temple personnel were housed across the street (pl. XX, fig. 2). The buttressed walls that mark it as a holy building and the bent-axis approach that builds up suspense before confronting the divine image are additional features derived from Mesopotamia. Unlike Mesopotamian temples, however, the actual cult building had low windows all around the façades; two can be seen flanking the main entrance on the left in pl. XXI. The court contained a free-standing room, possibly for ablutions, and a portico. The holy of holies, at the far end, was built out on a natural promontory so the windows were out of reach to the passerby. The same principle governed the layout of temples II and III in the upper city (pl. XXIII). On pl. XXII the base for the divine statue can be seen on the left, projecting into the stone-paved cella between two windowsills. Light, air and, perhaps, visual contact with nature surrounding the city were apparently felt to be indispensable to god as well as man. Some time during the Empire Period, perhaps as late as 1275-1250, the Hittites tripled the extent of their capital Hattusa by surrounding the adjoining hillside with 3 km of city walls, raised on an artificial ambankment. Two parabolic gateways provided access, protected by life-size high-relief figures that were meant to ward off evil: lions on the outside of the west gate and, on the inside of the east gate (now called 'royal gate'), a warrior god (pl. XXIV); between the two a raised gate was defended by sphinxes. In connection with the consummate modeling of this muscular figure—which is in sharp contrast to the flat relief of pls. XV-XVI—several scholars have quoted a letter from the Hittite king Hattusili III (ca. 1275-1250) to the king of Babylonia, asking the latter to send him an artist because he wants to set up images.[77] The only feature that might at all be connected to Babylonia is the helmet—here provided with the horns of divinity—from which a stocking-like streamer hangs down; similar headgear is worn by first-millennium Babylonian rulers.[78] The large features may be somewhat

[77] Frankfort, *AAAO*, p. 122; Bittel, *Les Hittites*, pp. 226-230; Benno Landsberger, *Sam'al* (Ankara, 1948), p. 113, note 269. Outside influence on this and other Hittite sculpture is disclaimed by J. V. Canby in *Oriens Antiquus* 15 (1976), pp. 33-42.

[78] E.g., Frankfort, *AAAO*, pls. 120-121; André Parrot, *Assur* (Paris, 1961), figs. 215-217.

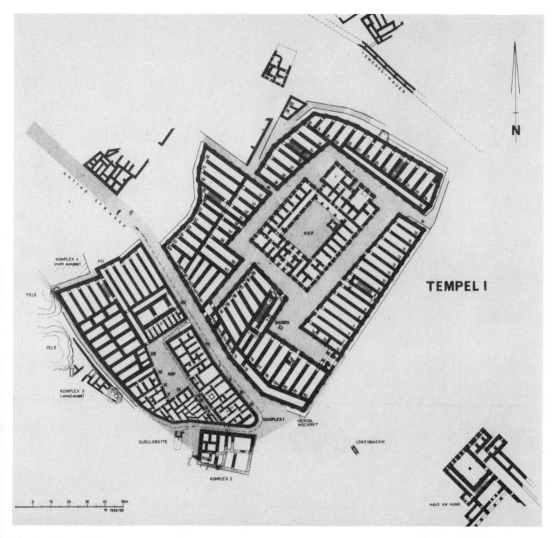

Fig. 2. Plan of Temple I, Bogazköy, 1275-1250. After K. Bittel & P. Neve in *MDOG* 102 (1970), fig. 1.

Syrian-inspired (compare the wide eyes and mouth of the Latakia statuette, pl. XLIIIc, with that from Hattusa itself, pl. XLIIIb). For the rest, the stance is typically Anatolian, with frontal torso and side-view legs bent in at the knees and planted far apart. The left fist is raised in a greeting or blessing gesture, but the right hand clasps a spiked battle axe, ready for action against evildoers. In addition, a crescent-hilted dagger is tucked into his wide belt. It is 'folded' along the body and onto the background, like the scimitars on pl. XXXIIIb. Close inspection reveals a wealth of engraved detail: curly hair on the chest with whorls around the nipples, herringbone and running-spiral designs on the kilt. Since (an image of) Suwaliyat or Tasmisu, brother of the storm god, is mentioned along with female sphinxes (?) among the points in public buildings that receive offerings, Güterbock has suggested the relief represents that militant junior god.[79]

[79] *RHA* 19 (1961), no. 68, pp. 15-16.

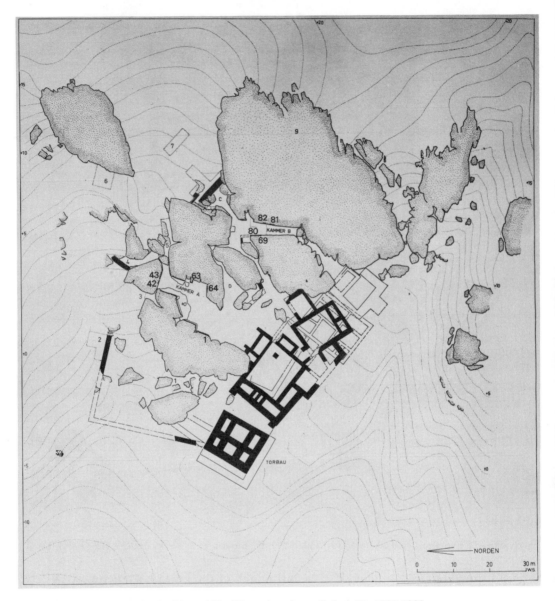

Fig. 3. Plan of Yazilikaya locating reliefs 1-82, 1250-1200.

A wealth of iconographic information is supplied by a series of 86 rock reliefs in the open-air sanctuary of Yazilikaya, 1.6 km northeast of Boğazköy, Turkey (ancient Hattusa, capital of the Hittites). The group of limestone outcrops, covering about one hectare and rising steeply to about 20 m above the hillside, must have inspired religious awe from early times, especially on account of the vertical clefts that created narrow passages between them. The two longest passages are labeled chamber A and chamber B; chamber A is 4-13, chamber B only 2-4 m wide (fig. 3).

The architectural additions can be dated as follows:[80]

Phase   I, *ca.* 1500 B.C.: area in front of chamber A surrounded by terrace wall.

Phase   II, *ca.* 1250 B.C.: temple with steps, altar and free-standing room in court, more rooms around court, and portico leading into chamber A, which apparently served as an open-air cella. King Tudhaliya IV is the putative author of this major constructive phase.

Phase III, *ca.* 1225 B.C.: gatehouse and outer wall added. Chamber B adapted to cult of dead king Tudhaliya IV.

Phase IV, *ca.* 1200 B.C.: east wing of temple replaced by second temple-like structure giving access to chamber B.

Rudolf Naumann has convincingly argued that the chamber A reliefs (pl. XXV-XXXIIIa) must belong to Phase II and the chamber B reliefs (pls. XXXIIIb-XXXVII) to Phase III. To the latter group I would also attribute relief 64 in chamber A (pl. XXXIV), representing Tudhaliya IV raised on two mountains, i.e. deified after his death.[81] Reliefs 36-37 in chamber A (pl. XXIXb) were recarved at some point before 1200 B.C. after the original carving, which was probably similar, had split off through natural causes.[82]

   All over ancient western Asia New Year's day seems to have been celebrated by taking the gods' statues a short distance into the country where the city's supreme deity would hold court and the citizens would enjoy an outdoor feast, much like the modern Turkish *ziyaret* still combines features of a nature sanctuary and a favorite pick-nick spot. Heinrich Otten has pointed to a Hittite text which may have a bearing on the original function of Yazilikaya:[83]

'For the thunder god a tremendous feast of heaven and earth was celebrated at the beginning of the year. All the gods assembled and entered the thunder god's house.' Texts concerning a spring festival also mention a procession to a locality outside of the capital.[84] The relief of chamber A then, like most of ancient architectural decoration, depicts the occasion at which this area fulfilled its purpose: a festive gathering of gods and goddesses,

---

[80] Rudolf Naumann in *HFY*, pp. 120-124. At the time when "1250 B.C. or shortly thereafter" was proposed for phase II, Tudhaliya IV, who was held responsible for that phase, was thought to have reigned *ca.* 1250 B.C. Now, however, it appears that his father Hattusili III was still alive in the 42nd year of Ramses II = 1238 B.C., see E. Edel, *Ägyptische Ärzte und ägyptische Medizin am hethitischen Königshof* (Opladen, 1976), p. 29, and E. F. Wente & C. C. van Siclen in *Studies in Honor of G. R. Hughes* (SAOC 39, Chicago, 1976), pp. 217-263. King Tudhaliya IV corresponded with Shalmaneser I of Assyria before 1234 B.C., J. A. Brinkman, *Materials and Studies for Kassite History I* (Chicago, 1976), pp. 31 and 7, note 4 and J. Boese & G. Wilhelm in *WZKM* 71 (1979), pp. 19-38. Rather than bringing the dates for Phases II-IV even closer together, I have let them stand, which implies that authorship for Phase II and the chamber A reliefs may have to be attributed to Hattusili III and his influential wife Puduhepa, daughter of a Hurrian priest. For Puduhepa's unique character and role in Hittite cultural history, see H. Otten, *Puduhepa: Eine hethitische Königin in ihren Textzeugnissen*, Mainz, 1975.
Its remains equally possible, of course, to attribute the chamber A reliefs to Tudhaliya IV (as Naumann *loc. cit.* intended) by dating Phase II *ca.* 1230, Phase III *ca.* 1210 and Phase IV *ca.* 1190 B.C.

[81] Hans G. Güterbock in *HFY*, p. 187.

[82] Kurt Bittel in *HFY*, p. 250.

[83] *OLZ* 51 (1956), pp. 101-102.

[84] Hans G. Güterbock in André Finet, ed., *Actes de la XVIIe Rencontre Assyriologique Internationale* (Ham-sur-Heure, 1970), p. 178.

arranged in the order that they were given in the Hurrian pantheon.[85] King Tudhaliya IV, grandson of a Hurrian priest and probable author of the reliefs, did much to institutionalize religion in the Hittite Empire along Hurrian lines. Although written with Luwian hieroglyphs, the inscriptions that float above the deities' greeting fists give their Hurrian names—which is not to say that the images may not represent their Hattic, Nesian or Luwian counterparts as well.

The male gods, proceeding from the left (pls. XXVI-XXXIIb), are headed by the thunder god, who on the central panel (pls. XXX-XXXI) meets and greets his wife and children. They in turn head the procession of goddesses (pls. XXXIIc-XXXIIIa) that approach from the right.

Fig. 4. Reliefs 16a-19, Yazilikaya, ca. 1250 B.C.

At the tail end of the male procession come twelve beardless gods in kilts, boots and single-horned pointed caps, shouldering scimitars (pl. XXVIa; for clearer details see chamber B reliefs 69-80 on pl. XXXIIIb). The overlapping figures and lifted back feet suggest soldiers marching in closed ranks. The twelve marching gods recur opposite the huge image of the Netherworld god in chamber B and a ritual text confirms that they belong to the retinue of this major deity.[86]

The next six figures (13-17) represent deified mountains, an important category among the numerous nature deities of Anatolia (pls. XXVIa, right, XXVIb, left). Five of them are bearded and rise as a human torso out of a mountain, rendered by the scale pattern

---

[85] Emmanuel Laroche, "Le panthéon de Yazilikaya," *JCS* 6 (1952), pp. 115-123. In *Oriens Antiquus* 13 (1974), pp. 211-226, V. Haas and M. Wäfler argued that Yazilikaya served mostly for purification rites, but H. G. Güterbock has countered their arguments in *JNES* 34 (1975), pp. 273-277.

[86] Hans G. Güterbock in *HFY*, p. 191.

that indicated rocky country elsewhere in Western Asia as well.[87] Four thorns, of as yet unexplained significance, stick out of the mountain on either side. At times they are pointed (pl. XXVIa), at times wavy (pl. XXXIV, upper left). Perhaps they simply portray the outline of a mountain, seen sideways. The front two mountain gods have their caps bent forward and both fists raised as if ready to fight (fig. 4).[88] One is reminded of the Hurrian myth of the thunder god fighting and defeating half-mountainous champions of an older generation of gods.[89] A gold bowl from west Iran, dating to about 1000 B.C. and apparently illustrating this myth, shows the mountain god with fists similarly raised.[90] This gesture seems different from that of the goddesses (pls. XXXI right, XXXIIc-XXXIIIa), who stick their right fist forward in greeting and raise the fingers of their left hand in prayer, and also from that of the straight-capped ivory mountain god (pl. XLId), who clasps his hands in a traditional Mesopotamian attitude of prayer.[91] The "boxing" attitude only occurs on the bent-capped gods on pls. XXVIb, XXVIIa and XXX, and I would interpret them as vanquished champions of the older generation of gods, their former agressiveness (or perhaps their present submission?) indicated by the raised fists, and their defeat and punishment indicated by the bent caps. For the figures that serve to support the thunder god on pl. XXX, Güterbock has suggested identification with Namni and Hazzi, the mountains at the mouth of the Orontes.[92] Since figure 17 on pl. XXVIb seems to be inscribed Na(m)ni,[93] it seems quite possible that the same mountain gods who serve as mounts on pl. XXX reappear here in their own right.

On pl. XXVIIa, every second god wears a cloak that envelops the right leg but leaves a kilt visible on the left thigh. One border hangs down from left elbow to left boot. The simultaneous portrayal of cloak and kilt, rarely seen on humans beings,[94] apparently serves to indicate a combination of dignity and readiness to fight that is characteristic of the gods. In Neo-Assyrian art it became the regular dress of supernatural beings.[95]

Scimitars, as carried by the two left-hand gods on pl. XXVIIb, seem to occur only on deities connected with death (including, perhaps, the death of game): on pls. XXVIa and XXXIIIb, the twelve gods; on pl. XXVIIb, second from left, the Netherworld god; on pl. XXVIIIa, war god Hesue, and on pl. XXVIIIc, war god Astabi. For this reason a close connection may exist between the two left-hand gods on pl. XXVIIb. The first one from the left is apparently inscribed Pisa(i)sap(hi). The Netherworld god's name is written with the logogram "sword".[96]

---

[87] See, e.g., *AAAO*, pp. 56, 72, pls. 45 D, 56, 65, 72, 76 A.

[88] The drawing in *HFY*, pl. 56, shows figure 17 with one opened hand, like the goddesses (figures 43, 45-63). The description, *HFY*, pp. 130-31, however, does not mention this feature; the photograph, *HFY*, pl. 15: 4, is equivocal.

[89] See note 59.

[90] See note 60.

[91] See, e.g., *AAAO*, pls. 9 B, 10, 13-17, 20 B, 22 C-24, 46-47, 57, 60-61.

[92] *HFY*, p. 170. Hazzi is classical Mons Casius and identical to Phoenician Ṣaphon, see W. Röllig, *RLA* 4 (Berlin, 1972-1975), pp. 241-242. Namni has not been localized as yet.

[93] The new readings proposed by Emilia Masson, *Le Panthéon de Yazilikaya* (Paris, 1981), are hard to verify on the basis of the photographs presented. Closer scrutiny is evidently needed before the scholars involved can reach a consensus.

[94] E.g., on an 18th-16th century victory stela in the Louvre, James B. Pritchard, *The Ancient Near East in Pictures* (2nd ed., Princeton, 1969), no. 308.

[95] *KAF*, pp. 29-30, pl. 1: 6-8.

[96] Güterbock in *HFY*, pp. 176-177. The name of his Babylonian equivalent, Nergal, is also written with the logogram "sword", but his Hurrian name has not been established as yet.

As we can see from Hurrian god lists, four deities must be included in the composition on the right of pl. XXVIIb: Heaven and Earth each represented by its ideogram, and the deified bulls Seri and Hurri that, like the Greek Atlas, prevent collision of these two elements. The common West Asian motif of the bull-man, with bull's horns and ears, human face and torso and bull's hindlegs and tail occurs in Hittite art as well (pl. XLIIc). In view of the Hurrians' liking for animal features in religious imagery, it would not be surprising to find bulls' faces here; Bittel interprets the remaining traces as such. On either side, however, pigtails of human hair stand out, as visible behind the elbows of most other gods.

Of the next group of four, three gods shoulder scimitars (pls. XXVIIIa, c). The foremost's name is written phonetically as that of the war god Astabi. The one to his left in pl. XXVIIIc has his name written half logographically, half phonetically as STAG/ANTLER-ti/di. Several readings have been proposed, including the name of the prominent Hurrian god Nubadig. The stag is the animal of protective gods in general, and of the protective god of the chase in particular. On Old Anatolian cylinder seals, the god of the chase occasionally rides on a stag (pl. IXa) and regularly shoulders what is usually interpreted as a crook or a boomerang rather than a scimitar (pl. VIIIb). In effect there seems to be less of an angle between hilt and blade in pl. XXVIIIc on the left than, e.g., in pl. XXVIIIc on the right. Another prominent Hurrian god, the war god Hesue, is unaccounted for as yet. Since war gods are occasionally described as carrying severed human heads, his name is probably to be sought behind the logogram "human head" on pl. XXVIIIa.[97] Finally, pl. XXVIIIb has the rounded to cylindrical cap of the goddesses (cf. pl. XXIXb) and the wings of Sauska (pl. XXIXc). Although the name cannot be read as yet, identification with Pirinkar, a variant form of war goddess Sauska, is likely.[98] We will dwell below on the reason for including these goddesses among the gods.

After pls. XXVIIb-XXVIIIc, which are on a diagonal stretch of rock wall, one turns a corner into the narrower inner part of chamber A. Here, the important deities of pl. XXIXa are on the left, with rock-cut libation gutter and basin in front of them. In Hittite iconography the sun god "of the sky" is assimilated to the king, who is addressed as "my sun" and also refers to himself as such. Iconographically, at least, he is undistinguishable from the king (cf. pl. XXXIV), except for the fact that he actually wears the winged sun disk on his head, whereas the king includes it in the cartouche or *aedicula* giving his name and titles. Unique to pl. XXIXa left, is the square inscribed within the crook. Is this also to be understood logographically, e.g., as spelling 'shepherd of the four corners of the earth?' The position of the crook, held down, is normal on portrayals of the king. Even today one can see shepherds retrieving wayward sheep with the hooked end of their crook. Perhaps readiness to redress human recalcitrance is implied. Although the crescent-shaped hilt of a dagger is visible at the king's waist, a large cloak enveloping the whole body, including the right arm, prevents any quick action and is suited most of all to ceremonial such as the king's many religious duties. Neo-Assyrian kings later wear closely wrapped garments only when performing religious duties.[99] The hemispherical cap might

---

[97] See preceding note.
[98] Güterbock in *HFY*, p. 175.
[99] *KAF*, pp. 37-38, pl. 2.

be compared to the caps worn by Neo-Sumerian and Old-Babylonian royalty.[100] The moon god is once more depicted in the normal guise of a bearded god with kilt and small cloak. The moon crescent is placed across his pointed cap and wings grow out of his shoulders.

As mentioned above, the two deities appearing on pl. XXIXb have been recarved after damage to an original that may, however, been similar to the surviving relief. With their shallowly modeled breasts and long pleated skirts they are clearly female. One carries a mirror, the other an ointment horn. Their insertion among the gods is a consequence of the bisexual character of their mistress Sauska, the planet Venus, visible at dawn and dusk, that inspires man to war and love. She immediately precedes them (pl. XXIXc), and the ambiguity of her character is expressed by her head, torso and left leg being those of a male deity, whereas her back leg is enveloped in a pleated skirt.[101] On the other goddesses (pls. XXIXb, XXXI, XXXIId-XXXIIIa) the pleats fall down, with the lower part drawn backward by the dragging train. At most they describe a double curve, with the front part blown back horizontally before falling down, perhaps implying movement through the sky (pls. XXXIIc, Nikkal on pl. XXXIIIa). Certainly the upward curving pleats on pl. XXIXc imply the swift movement of winged Sauska when she intervenes on the battlefield.

Sauska in turn is preceded by the water god Ea, visible at the right on pl. XXIXa. The procession then makes another right angle and the next god, Kumarbi (pl. XXXIIa) appears on the back wall of the open-air cella, in accordance with his rank as chief of the older generation of gods, now unseated by his son Tesub. The higher rank of the gods on the back wall is also brought out by placing them on truncated conical mountains and/or animal mounts. Above Kumarbi's fist is the ear of grain that characterizes him as the grain god. The next god's hieroglyphs call him Lord of ... (pl. XXXIIb). The deity normally mentioned between Tesub and Kumarbi is Tesub's brother Tasmisu, equivalent of Babylonian Ninurta who vanquished the lion-eagle Anzu. In addition to dagger and mace, he holds a tall staff; its bottom is visible below a large hole in the rock. His pointed cap is surmounted by a tiny crouching bull. One is reminded of the lightning god with his spear on a lion-eagle that accompanies the thunder god on his bull in pl. Vc.

The supreme god (pl. XXX) is shown at least a head taller than his brother. His pointed cap has four rows of horns; the two center rows almost meet to form a row of buckle-shaped "god" hieroglyphs. He shoulders a huge mace and above his greeting fist are the hieroglyphs "god, lightning". Behind him a calf, also wearing the gods' pointed cap, is frolicking in such a way that his head and rearing forelegs are visible to the right, and his raised tail to the left of the thunder god (fig. 5). Hieroglyphs expressly label him "Tesub's calf". The thunder god's feet rest on the arched backs of the two deified mountains that have been discussed in our treatment of pl. XXVIb.

What impresses the modern visitor to Yazilikaya most of all is the extraordinary sense of harmony achieved by the ancient sculptor in the central scene, despite a certain clum-

---

[100] See, e.g., *AAAO*, pls. 41, 48-49, 53-54a, 61, 63-65.

[101] On a 17th-century Syrian seal, it looks as if she has one female and one male breast, *CANES* I, no. 958. Such images may have given rise to the legend of the Amazons. On Sauska's iconography see also M. J. Mellink in Kurt Bittel et al., eds., *Vorderasiatische Archäologie ... Anton Moortgat* (Berlin, 1964), pp. 155-164.

Fig. 5. Reliefs 42-43, *ca.* 1250 B.C.

siness in execution, for instance, of the eagle's claws (pl. XXXI, right). In part it is due
to the slanting plane, which draws man's eye up to rock summit and sky, but permits the
gods to descend from their distant abodes; in part to the fact that the ancient sculptor has
expressed the complementarity of man and woman, god and goddess in universally
understandable visual terms. Authority and vigilance are hinted at by caps and cloaks,
maces and daggers; but most of all the innate propensities of the male are expressed by
squared shoulders, swinging elbows, swelling thighs and calves, and feet planted wide
apart. In utter contrast to these are the flowing forms, the conciliating gestures of the goddesses. Here it is not militance and dignity, it is subservience and dignity between which
the sculptor must strike a balance. Rigidly straight in her stance, Hebat seems to lower
her head ever so slightly on its forward-stretched neck (pl. XXX, right). Her ankle-length

plait follows this movement of neck and shoulders. The facial features, with short, straight nose and small, pursed lips are decidedly less Near Eastern than the possibly Syro-Anatolian faces we have seen before (pls. IVb, XXIV). The greeting gesture of the right fist does not differ from that of the gods, but the left fingers are raised, pleading for all those who have prayed to her. Both arms are enveloped in a loose bodice or wrap with tiny vertical pleats. Below the wide belt the skirt falls in much larger, widely spaced pleats. The hem falling from right elbow to right boot shows that, as in Babylonia, women wrapped their garments clockwise starting from the right elbow, not counterclockwise starting from the left elbow as did the men. Her simple earring is identical to that of gods and king, but the three-turreted crown is reserved for major goddesses (cf. her daughter and grand-daughter on the double eagle, Hutena and Hutellura, pl. XXXIId, and Nikkal on pl. XXXIIIa). The other goddesses seem to wear a turretless cylindrical crown with vertical pleats. Behind Hebat another calf, counterpart to Tesub's bull calf, is frolicking while her feet rest on a slender leonine creature[102] that I am calling a lioness. A similar creature, that I call a lion cub, supports her son Sarruma. The association immediately calls to mind the great Anatolian mother goddess, enthroned on or between leonine mounts, that appears at Çatalhüyük around 6000 B.C. and is worshipped as late as Roman times. We have seen her on Old Anatolian seals seated on leonine supports and surrounded by other animals (pls. IXb-c). Certainly the Hurrian-inspired supreme goddess of Yazilikaya is not the same we see disrobing and dispensing rain as consort of the thunder god on Old Anatolian seals.

We have yet to deal with the male and female offspring of Tesub and Hebat, portrayed to her right in the main scene (pl. XXXI). The young god Sarruma, shouldering an axe, holds his mount by a leash. In deference to his father he is here shown with six horns down the front of his cap, but on pl. XXXV, where he takes on a major role as protector of the king, he wears four rows of at least six horns each. The goddesses with turreted crowns that follow him and float above a double eagle are identified as Alanzu, daughter of Tesub and Hebat, and 'Tesub's granddaughter', whose Hurrian name is not known as yet.

After a gap the procession of goddesses continues, first at a sharp angle, then at right angles to the main scene, along the right wall. We have chosen the goddess Hutellura, better preserved than most, as representative of goddesses 46a-48 (pl. XXXIId). She was preceded by Hutena. Each of the two actually stands for a whole group of fate goddesses. Turrets on their crowns indicate their importance. Not much more needs to be said about the remaining goddesses, here represented by figures 50-55 (pl. XXXIIIa) except that Nikkal, wife of the moon god, seems to be singled out by a turreted crown (?), wind-blown skirt and by a rock-cut offering table in front of her, corresponding to the rock-cut libation basin in front of her husband (pl. XXIXa). The stone on pl. XXXIIc was found reused at Yekbas north of Yazilikaya. It shows a goddess with slightly wind-blown skirt, such as would fit a celestial goddess. According to a suggestion of Bittel's,[103] it may have filled the gap between figures 55 and 56 together with one other relief figure. The inscription on pl. XXXIIc shows the female Sauska must have been the missing figure. To the right of the entrance to chamber A the rock wall facing the main scene has been carved with

---

[102] See Wolf Herre, quoted by Kurt Bittel, *HFY*, p. 250, note 6.
[103] *HFY*, p. 145.

a relief (pl. XXXIV) portraying king Tudhaliya IV raised on two mountains after he had 'become a god' (such was the Hittite euphemism for a king's death).[104] In another common parlance the Hittite king is likened to the sun god. His titles, rendered by the hieroglyphs in the upper left,[105] begin with 'my sun (the winged sun disk)', much as we would say 'my majesty'. In the rest of his appearance he is identical to the sun god on pl. XXIXa (see the discussion of that plate for details), but this is due to assimilation of the sun god's iconography to the king's and not the other way around. It is not likely that the king wore these cumbersome ceremonial clothes for the more mundane and martial enterprises which he also must have pursued. But the frequence with which he is shown in such priest-like ceremonial dress, with only long robe and crook distinguishing him as a king (cf. pls. XVb-c), may reflect the kings' preoccupation with religious duties which also transpires from the texts.

At the far (north) end of chamber B a slab of 1.40 × 1.40 m was found on what must have been the floor. With some socket-like stones found nearby it may have formed the base of a statue, presumably the focus of the dead king's cult. An isolated *aedicula* with the name of Tudhaliya, carved on the adjoining eastern rock wall, may have served as label to the statue. Three low niches, up to 1.60 m wide, carved out of the east and west rock walls, could have served to lay the king's bones, and those of relatives, to rest after cremation. The ritual speaks of placing the bones on a bed in his stone house, with an oil lamp by the bed.[106] In the adjoining chamber C another stone base (for an altar?) was still surrounded by much ash and bones of cattle, sheep and goats as well as hare, falcon and eagle. A curious find was made by the excavators in crevice D, between chambers A and B: here a pig embryo had been nailed into the earth by four bronze pegs, covered with a bowl laid upside down and surrounded by ten more pegs. Undoubtedly the impurities of someone to be cleansed had thus been consigned to the Netherworld.[107]

Just as the chamber A reliefs reflect the gathering of the gods that was celebrated there, the chamber B reliefs (pls. XXXIIIb, XXXV-XXXVII) indicate that one prayed to the Netherworld gods here, imploring their mercy for the dead king Tudhaliya IV. We see the latter entering the presence of the Hurrian Hades on pl. XXXV. The king is led and at the same time protectively embraced by the much taller figure of Sarruma, the god we have seen as a boy on pl. XXXI, but who here acts as a Hurrian Hermes Psychopompos. They both direct their right fist, with thumb on top, in greeting toward the towering image of Hell. Above are the hieroglyphs spelling the names, left, of the god, right, of the

---

[104] See note 81.
[105] The following elements compose the *aedicula*:

		SUN		
GREAT	LA-	MOUN-	LA-	GREAT
	BAR-	TAIN	BAR-	
	NA	GOD	NA	
KING	+ la	+ tu	+ la	KING

to be read "my sun Tudhaliya (originally the name of a holy mountain), the Labarna (a title), the great king."

[106] Heinrich Otten, *Hethitische Totenrituale* (Berlin, 1958), p. 14.
[107] See Harald Hauptmann in *HFY*, pp. 64-70.

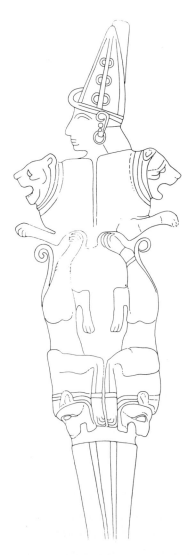

Fig. 6. Relief 82, Yazilikaya, *ca.* 1225 B.C.

king.[108] This touching expression of faith can be appreciated even better from a plaster cast which was taken before recent damage to the king's face (pl. XXXVI).

Hell itself is one of the most complex images at Yazilikaya (pl. XXXVII). The god's intermediate rank is indicated by the presence of seven horns on his cap—one in front and three pairs down the center (fig. 6). His beardless head rises out of the elaborate hilt of a greatly enlarged dagger, the point of which is stuck into the ground. The blade has the ribs or 'blood-rills' typical of Syrian and Anatolian daggers from about 1750 to 1200 B.C.[109] The hilt includes two complete lions, hanging down and, as it were, spitting out

[108] See note 105. This time Tudhaliya is spelt MOUNTAIN × GOD + tu, and the logogram HERO is added to the titles.

[109] Rachel Maxwell-Hyslop in *Iraq* 8 (1946), pp. 1-65, types 26b, 12a. Her type 11 includes early lion hilts.

the blade. They are surmounted, at right angles, by two lion protomes back to back. Two lions decorate the hilt of a sword with a 19th-18th century B.C. dedication to the Netherworld god, said to have been found in southeast Turkey.[110] In Neo-Assyrian times four lions decorate the swords of king and crown prince.[111]

On the rock wall opposite the Netherworld god are pictured the twelve marching gods, armed with scimitars, that belong to his retinue (pl. XXXIIIb). Having been glazed by a natural lime deposit, the figures on this relief are much better preserved than in chamber A (pl. XXVIa). A feature present on all male figures, but particularly striking here, may require elucidation: the bunch in the male figures' necks is not, as one might think, a muscle stretching the neck forward, but simply hair falling down behind the squared shoulder and reappearing, wherever there is room to show it, as a pigtail behind the elbow (cf. pl. XXXVI).

Two lion demons guard the entrance to chamber B. With their opened jaws and raised claws they threaten anyone who might approach the narrow passage with evil intentions. Lion- and eagle-headed demons were among the supernatural beings in animal form so dear to the Hurrians. Later they reappear in Neo-Assyrian palace reliefs, where the lion demons specifically have the function of threatening evildoers.[112]

Kurt Bittel has suggested a date toward 1200 B.C. for a curious monument in the southwest of the Hittite Empire that one might consider a man-made rock facade (pl. XXXIX).[113] It overlooked a spring that has now been dammed to form a lake. The large upper sun disk must have been completed by another block, now missing. It is supported on either side by two genii, perhaps lion-headed above and bull-legged below, and frames two similar compositions which in turn serve to frame a frontal sitting god and goddess. Although badly weathered, the god can be seen to have worn a tall, tapering cap and the goddess a halo-like beret. An ivory carved with a comparable human pyramid of Hittite figures has been found at Megiddo, Palestine, in a palace destroyed about 1150 B.C.[114]

A similar tall cap, tapering (not pointed) and provided with four horns down the front, crowns the storm god on the gigantic stele found abandoned on a hillside not far away (pl. XXXVIII). To explain its unfinished look, Hans Güterbock has suggested that it was being dragged from the limestone quarry to its final destination.[115] Perhaps hostilities marking the end of the Hittite Empire interrupted the work. The young god, ready to smite with his lightning, stands on a mountain god who joins his hands in prayer and is flanked by two lions.

Several scholars have used Hittite texts describing divine images to identify iconographical themes with specific deities, but a one-to-one correspondence between

---

[110] Hans G. Güterbock in *Studies in Honor of Benno Landsberger* (Assyriological Studies 16, Chicago, 1965), pp. 197-198.

[111] *KAF*, pp. 86-87, pl. 21: 16-22.

[112] Julian E. Reade in *Baghdader Mitteilungen* 10 (1979), pp. 39-40. They brandish daggers and appear in doorways.

[113] *Les Hittites*, p. 222.

[114] Gordon Loud, *The Megiddo Ivories* (OIP 52, Chicago, 1939) pl. 11.

[115] *In Memoriam Halil Edhem* (TTKY V:5, Ankara, 1947) I, pp. 59-70, quoted by James Mellaart in *Anat St* 12 (1962), pp. 111-117. Mellaart suggests a stela like it may have been intended to crown the monument on pl. XXXIX. Bittel thinks it unlikely that a stela crowned the sun disk of pl. XXXIX; see however, our pl. XLIIc and Winfried Orthmann's reconstruction in Kurt Bittel et al., eds., *Vorderasiatische Archäologie... Anton Moortgat* (Berlin, 1964), pp. 221-229.

description and monument found is rare.[116] Most of the relevant texts have been dated to the reign of Tudhaliya IV (*ca.* 1225 B.C.) and take the form of cult inventories; some record the results of a major renovation of divine images by this pious king. Besides human figures, animal figures, animal-shaped vessels, vessels in the shape of breast, scrotum or fist, simple vessels, horns, weapons and sun disks as well as standing stones could all represent the deity. These standing stones, usually outside of the city, can carry a human image and therefore include relief stelae. In other instances they are contrasted to anthropomorphic images that the same god can have in a city temple. Most cities listed have a storm god, a sun goddess, male mountain gods and female spring and river deities. After Tudhaliya's reform most deities had anthropomorphic images except for the storm god, for whom a new bull statuette had often been made. The statuettes, mostly out of precious metal (including iron), rarely exceeded a cubit (*ca.* 50 cm) in height.

Below we quote in full some particularly relevant descriptions, to give an idea of the amount of detail, and of uncertainties, that the texts contain:[117] "Sauska..., sitting, [wings coming] out of her shoulder blade, in her right hand [she holds] a beaker of gold, [in her left hand] she holds "well-being" of gold; beneath her there is a silver-plated pedestal; [beneath] the pedestal [however] lies a silver-plated *awiti*;[118] right [and left] of the *awiti*'s wings, however, stand Ninatta and Kulitta in silver, their eyes gold-plated; be-[neath] the *awiti* however, there is a wooden pedestal. A handful of bread to them daily and an earthenware beaker of wine, Ninatta and Kulitta included; a monthly feast and a song for them. She doesn't have a priest. (There is) one gold vessel (in the shape of) a bull's (head and) neck."

"City Wiyanawanta: god protecting the wild [fields, the cult statue] is a statuette of a man in gold, [sta]nding, with a helmet (??),[119] in his right hand he holds a gold bow, [in his] left [hand] he holds a gold eagle and a gold hare; a gold dagger—there is gold "fruit" on it—; he stands on a gold stag that stands on all fours."

"City of Lapana: Iyaya, the cult statue is the statuette of a woman in wood, sitting, veiled, of one [span], her head gold-plated but her body and her throne tin-plated. Two tin-plated wooden wild sheep sit below the goddess right and left; one tin-plated eagle,

---

[116] Carl G. von Brandenstein, *Hethitische Götter nach Bildbeschreibungen...* (MVAeG 46: 2), Leipzig, 1943. Liane Jakob-Rost in *MIO* 8 (1963), pp. 161-217, 9 (1963), pp. 175-239. Hans G. Güterbock in *Belleten* 7 (1943), pp. 295-317, in *Orientalia* N.S. 15 (1946), pp. 482-496 and in *BAK*, pp. 203-217. Dr. Güterbock kindly sent me the latter article in manuscript before it appeared.

[117] Jakob-Rost in *MIO* 8 (1963), pp. 175, 179-180, 181.

[118] This word designating Sauska's animal is translated as "fabulous creature, sphinx" by Güterbock with reference to the Konya ring, here pl. XLVId. Another name for the sphinx has plausibly been suggested by him as well, see note 79. The dove is the favored animal of the Syro-Anatolian love goddess, as stated in discussing pl. IIc above.

[119] The word designating the god's apparel is left untranslated by Güterbock. It is associated with armor, with the Netherworld god, and with priests. A meaning that would fit the first association is "helmet." In *BAK*, p. 206, Güterbock has suggested that the designation *hupitauwanza* applies to the apparel and, possibly, to the headgear in particular (veil?) of female cult statues. By analogy I am suggesting that the designations *kurudawanza* and *lupannauwanza* apply to the apparel and, specifically, to the headgear of male cult statues. Since *lupanni-* means "turban" or "cap" and *lupannauwanza* apparently "turbaned" or "capped," *kurudawan-za* might mean "helmeted." All these words are Luwian neuter singulars in agreement with the word for "statue."

Table 1

Name or type of deity	Shape of cult image	Posture	Right hand holding	Left hand holding	Standing or sitting on	Apparel	Other attributes
Gods:							
Hanakka	man	standing					
Iskisa (a mountain god)	man	standing	mace	shield, eagle and lion			*kunziyala* engraved with wild animals
Kalli	man	standing			mountain		
Karmahili	man	sitting	mace		pedestal		dagger
"Lord of lords"?	man	standing					
Other mountain gods	mace (12 ×)/ man (6 ×)	standing			2 springs (2 ×)/lion (1 ×)		often image and/or sun disk and moon crescent on mace
Patron gods	shield (1 ×)/ man (2 ×)	standing	spear	shield	pedestal		
Patron gods of nature	man	standing	bow	eagle and hare	stag	helmet??	dagger
Companion of latter?	man	standing			winged creature on rein	turban	
Patron god of the spear	man	standing					
Plague god	man	standing			lion		
Santa?	man	standing					
Sauska as war god	winged man	standing	axe	"well-being"	winged creature		attendants Ninatta and Kulitta
Storm gods	man (4 ×)/bull or bull rhyton (11 ×)	standing			pedestal (2 ×)	armor	mace, sword (1 ×)
Storm god of heaven	man (1 ×)/ bull (1 ×)	sitting	mace	"well-being"	2 mountain gods, pedestal		
Storm god-hero	man	standing			pedestal	armor	
Storm god of the (royal) house	bull	standing (1 ×)/ kneeling (1 ×)			pedestal		
Sun god of heaven	man	sitting			pedestal	"fish" (wings) on head	

Name or type of deity	Shape of cult image	Posture	Right hand holding	Left hand holding	Standing or sitting on	Apparel	Other attributes
Other war gods	man	standing	dagger (1×)/mace (1×)	man's head (1×)/shield (1×)	lion (2×), pedestal (1×)		shields, daggers (1×)
Zithariya	shield						
Goddesses:							
"Any deity"	woman	standing	grapes				
Anzili	woman	sitting	beaker				daughter on knees
Dam goddess	woman					veiled?	
Daughter of storm god	sun disk						
Daughter-in-law of storm god			beaker		pedestal	veiled?	
Grain goddess	woman	sitting				veiled?	
Horse goddess	woman?		?	whip	horse	rings, belt	
"Lady built-the-house"	woman						
Mother goddess	woman	sitting	beaker		2 wild sheep/pedestal	veiled?	eagle, 2 staffs
Mother goddess and baby	woman	sitting					baby
River goddesses	woman						
Sauska as love goddess	winged woman	sitting	beaker	"well-being"	pedestal, winged creature		attendants Ninatta and Kulitta
Spring goddesses	woman	sitting	beaker (1×)			earrings (1×)	sun disk (1×)/moon crescents (1×)
Sun Goddesses	woman (2×)/sun disk (2×)	sitting			pedestal, 2 wild sheep		10 rays
Wife of Hanakka	woman	sitting				veiled?	
Za(s)hapuna	woman	standing			mountain		
Zuliya	woman						

two copper staffs, two bronze beakers are present as utensils of the deity. She has a new temple; a male priest has been there from before.''

The textual information on cult statues is tabulated on pp. 30-31.[120] Not included in this table are the many standing stones and/or stelae that had traditionally been focuses of worship. The cult inventories often include storm god, sun goddess and 'patron god' (of nature) in the list of divine images for a given town. Güterbock has ingeniously compared this triad with the three silver and gold objects on plate XL, which were found together according to the dealer.[121] The stag and the bull are admirably modeled, but one can notice a certain predilection for Y-shaped veins, tripartite muscles and shield-shaped shoulder blades that recurs in more linear form on the stag hunt and bull worship reliefs from Alaca Höyük (cf. pl. XVd). The scene around the neck of the cup is to be read from right to left. First we see spears, quiver and water bag put aside after a successful hunt, in which a stag was killed. The three hunters, in short cloaks over cutaway kilts (cf. pls. XIIa, XIIIb, XVb-c) offer food and drink to the deities who have granted them the coveted game. The second hunter brings flat pebble-baked *pide* bread (as still eaten in Turkey), the third libates from a beaked pitcher into the ground (cf. pls. XIb, XVIIa). Before him the young hunting god, with crook and falcon, stands on a stag. Behind the boy god a goddess in a horned pointed cap sits on a folding stool before a (probably metal) censer, of a type hitherto not attested before the 12th century B.C.[122] Her right hand raises a drinking bowl, while a falcon is perched on her left fist. Obviously she is the hunting god's mother, and pl. XVIIa is to be similarly understood as showing mother and son. The loops on the front of the men's and woman's sandals link this scene with that on pl. XIIIc and point, along with the early Empire features already mentioned, to a date around 1400 B.C. The neck and handle of the cup on pl. XLc have been restored and may originally have carried another scene in relief. The muscle markings include the same horizontals on the cheek and verticals on the dewlap that pl. XVd shows in more linear form. Like the stag vessel, the bull vessel may have been used in the cult and, at the same time, may have served as the object of worship, i.e., the image of the deity. We see this, e.g., from a text listing divine images: 'Storm god of the (royal) house: a silver bull's neck, kneeling in front.'[123] The mother's huge beret on pl. XLd creates the effect of a halo and suggests her being the sun goddess, so important in Hittite religion. One should note, however, that berets were worn by other goddesses as early as the Colony Period (pl. IXc); in the Old Hittite and early Empire Period we have seen what may be large berets covered by a veil (pls. XIb, XVIIa) which, in side view, give the same tall pointed outline as the mother's 'halo'. Her right hand once held something, probably a drinking bowl, while her other hand reaches toward the baby on her knees. The baby seems to have a triangular pubic area and hands joined in front of the chest (cf. pl. Ia), but it is bald. Nevertheless, it is probably meant to represent a girl. Except for its size the figurine nicely

---

[120] Condensed from Jakob-Rost in *MIO* 9 (1963), pp. 204-209, with additions from Güterbock in *BAK*. As much as possible I have listed the deities by type rather than by name.
In translating "Lord of lords," "armor" and "veiled?" and in not translating the appearance of Hatepuna, Daughter-in-law of the Storm god, I have followed Güterbock.
[121] *BAK*, p. 217.
[122] Ursula Seidl in *Der alte Orient*, ill. 191 (in worship scene before a goddess).
[123] *BAK*, p. 213.

fits the above description of the statuette of Anzili. As it is, with a loop fixed to the back
of the goddess' headdress, it can only have served as a pendant. In these and later times,
Mesopotamians wore symbols of deities around the neck for protection.[124] A divine image
of gold, small enough to hang from a priest's necklace, would be easy to protect against
theft and could still be detached for purposes of worship.

Plates XLIa-c and XLIIa show more pendant divine images, varying from 2 to 3 cms
in height. The smallest cult statues listed in the inventories were one hand's width high.
The seated figure of pl. XLIb is generally considered a goddess, although she lacks the
halo and has huge ears as usually shown on gods and men (cf. P. XLId). The head is bare
except for a headband and the body is enveloped in a cloak from which the hands emerge
to hold a large bowl. As in many Hittite figures, the head is stretched forward, giving an
intent look which has led George Hanfmann to believe she (or he) is busying herself atten-
tively,[125] possibly stirring a brew.

The staff held by the god from Yozgat (pl. XLIa) looks as if it had been a crook of which
the loop has broken off. A crook hanging with the loop down is regularly held by sun god
and by king (pls. XVd, XXIXa), but occasionally by other gods as well (pls. XIa, XLIIa).
The Yozgat figure has a pointed cap with two pairs of horns against its sides, pointing
up and back in the fashion of goat's (not bull's) horns. The bull on pl. XLIc is humped,
as in pl. XLc, and like the latter probably represents the storm god. His horns are broken;
whisker-like markings, radiating from the mouth, indicate the cheek muscles (cf. pls.
XVd, XLc).

The tiny mountain god on pl. XLId has no suspension loop and must have been used
in some different way. In addition to two angular horns engraved on either side of his
pointed cap, there are five knobs down its front (rudimentary horns?, cf. pl. XXXVIII).
His body rises out of a mountain as on pls. XXVIa-b, XXX, etc. His hands are joined
with the thumbs on top in respectful greeting.

Plate XLIIa presents us with a unique scene, in which the central figure seems to have
his head inside a bull's mask (cf. pl. XIIIa). On either side are gods in tall caps tapering
to a rounded point somewhat like those on pls. XXXVIII-XXXIX. These large-eared
figures, draped in long cloaks, hold crooks with the loop down.

The little stela on pl. XLIIb is big enough to have served as a cult statue. The relief
theme accords well with the description of the hunting god (literally 'patron god of the
wild fields') in the texts quoted above, except that he here shoulders a crook, not a bow,
and lacks the hare. In various closely related guises we can recognize him from Colony
Period times (pls. VIa, VIIIb, IXa) down to the end of the Empire Period (pls. XLIVa-b,
XLVIe). That the patron god (apparently the protector of wildlife in particular) vied in
popularity with the storm god is implied by the existence of a myth according to which
the patron god once took the rule over heaven (symbolized by reins and whip) away from
Tesub. But apparently drought and famine set in, the animals of the earth rebelled and
the patron god had to recognize the storm god as his master.[126]

---

[124] Winfried Orthmann, *Der alte Orient*, ill. 253a (18th-16th century necklace said to come from Dilbat);
KFA, p. 56, pl. 9:6.
[125] *AJA* 66 (1962), p. 4.
[126] Güterbock, *MAW*, pp. 161-164.

In pl. XLIIc an aniconic stela rests upon a winged sun disk—which may also symbolize the sky[127]—supported by two bull-men. Despite their worn condition one can recognize their faces as human. They are obviously the same Atlas-like demigods that keep heaven and earth apart and appear after the celestial and before the chthonic deities at Yazilikaya (pl. XXVIIb). Here the bulls that serve as their mounts stand on a rectangle divided by grooves into blocks (mountains?).

A similar scene, including the central tree, is repeated several times on the outer band of pl. XLIId. Despite a certain clumsiness that makes the bull-men's legs and the bulls' horns (in the middle band) seem crooked the craftsman must have used a Hittite example of the 14th century B.C. The bulls display some of the same muscle markings as on pl. XVd.

Even in its present armless and legless state the impressive bronze god from Dogantepe (pl. XLIIIa) is certainly tall enough to have served as a cult statue. Grooves along the sides show it was originally silver- or gold-plated. The arms were made separately and riveted to the torso. The right shoulder seems slightly raised, as if he lifted his right arm. If this is so, we have another image of the popular 'smiting god,' raising the mace or spear of lightning. The bronze god from Hattusa, otherwise similar, still preserves his right arm (pl. XLIIIb). It is held away from the body at waist level, balancing the forward movement of the left leg. One short side of the wrapped loincloth shows as a diagonal fringe slightly overlapping his thigh, as on pl. XXIV. The similar statuette from Latakia (pl. XLIIIc) is remarkable for its broad face, which is a Syrian trait in this otherwise Hittite figure.

Miniature inlay figures of gods and demigods were made out of lapis lazuli, set in gold and apparently attached to clothing to protect the owner (pl. XLIVa, c-d were found in an Iron Age cremation grave at Carchemish).[128] Among them the hunting god appears twice: with bow and falcon at Carchemish (pl. XLIVa) and with throwing stick, hare and falcon at Assur. The Assur piece was found in the temple of Ishtar in a level predating 1250 B.C.[129] It is conceivable that the 'throwing stick' or boomerang was longer and resembled a crook originally.[130] The sun-god from Carchemish (pl. XLIVc), appropriately all in gold, has his crook awkwardly bent (cf. the king on pl. XVd). The bowknot on his fist is the Hittite 'life' sign, often strewn in the field of seals (e.g., pls. XIb, XLVb). Several of the Carchemish figures (pl. XLIVd) can be matched at Yazilikaya: the winged goddess of war and love with pl. XXIXc, the winged moon god with pl. XXIXa, and the goddess with, e.g., pl. XXXIIIa. One therefore wonders if the cremation grave in which they were found could perhaps date to the very end of the Bronze Age, when the Iron Age custom of cremating the dead began to spread from Anatolia into Syria.[131]

---

[127] Henri Frankfort, *Cylinder Seals* (London, 1939), pp. 207-215, 275-278.

[128] Sir Leonard Woolley & Richard D. Barnett, *Carchemish* III (London, 1952), pp. 250-257. A puzzling fact is that the grave is reported to belong to the end of the Iron Age occupation, toward 600 B.C. See, however, Ursula Seidl in *IstMitt* 22 (1972), pp. 15-43.

[129] Walter Andrae, *Die jüngeren Ischtar-Tempel* (WVDOG 58, Leipzig, 1935), p. 50.

[130] On throwing sticks etc. in ancient western Asia see W. Farber in *RLA* 3 (1957-71), pp. 250-252; Toufic Solyman, *Die Entstehung und Entwicklung der Götterwaffen* ... (Beirut, 1968), pp. 58, 110.

[131] As Ursula Seidl has pointed out in *IstMitt* 22 (1972), pp. 15-43, the four-handled krater from this grave is paralleled at Hama cremation cemetery I, 1200-1075 B.C., P. J. Riis, *Hama II:3* (Copenhagen 1948), pp. 59, 202.

The first imperial seal that we show (pl. XLVa) is also the earliest example of a motif that was repeated in stone at Yazilikaya (pl. XXXV): the king, dressed as usual as a high priest, is led by his god, labeled "Great Lightning of the sky". The towering deity protectively passes his right arm, still holding the thunderbolt mace, around the king's neck. The next imperial seal shows the supreme god, labeled "strong lightning god", once more in a protective pose, this time embracing his son and greeting his wife, the sun goddess, who appears on the left (pl. XLVb). The young god Sarruma shoulders a spear. Undoubtedly he is invoked because the king's name, appearing on a large scale below his throne name, is composed with the logogram spelling "Sarruma". Another seal of the same great king (pl. XLVd) gives his throne name in a more elaborate version, in which the sign MOUNTAIN × GOD is replaced by the detailed image of a mountain god, representing the holy mountain after which the successive Tudhaliyas were named. We clearly distinguish the pointed crown with three horns in front and three behind, the double pigtail, horizontally undulated beard, crescent-hilt dagger and scaly skirt with four thorns on either side (cf. pls. XXVIa-b, XXX, XXXIV). Tudhaliya is privileged among mountain gods in being armed and free to move his feet. His mace tends to make him into a god of the thunder on mount Tudhaliya.

Documents found in the burned palace of Ugarit have preserved imprints of some of the finest Hittite stamp seals, cylinder seals and signet rings. Ini-Tesub, a member of the junior branch of the imperial family installed as kings of Carchemish and viceroys of north Syria, had at least five seals. His stamp sealing is particularly well preserved and impressive (pl. XLVc). We now clearly see the storm god's lightning mace tucked under his right armpit. His pointed crown has three pairs of horns in front and three behind. The beardless sphinx whose forepaws he has caught in his left fist wears a crown with three horns. One wonders if this creature, that reached the Hittites from Syria, symbolizes Syria itself.[132] Ini-Tesub's cylinder sealing (pl. XLVIa) shows a combination of Anatolian themes (tall-crowned gods on their mounts) with Syrian motifs (lion hunt, griffin, stylized plants and water). The lightning god Tesub, on the bent backs of two mountain gods, with his calf gamboling behind him greet a young god that, if we go by pl. XXX, is his son Sarruma. The latter is supported by a kneeling eagle-headed genius, envoy from the earthly domain of his mother (see discussion of pl. XIIIc). Single combat with a lion is an old Mesopotamian device for testing the charisma that a king should possess. Since the lion killer stands on a bull, however, (and possibly also has a horn on the front of his round cap) we consider him to be another manifestation of the thunder-and-lightning god. A similar cylinder seal was used by an official at Ugarit who carried the Egyptian name of Amanmasu (Amun-mose), illustrating the international character of the age. Amun-Reᶜ being an Egyptian sun god, it is not surprising to find the Hittite sun god on his lion between the figures of Tesub and Sarruma. The latter now shoulders a bow and wields a staff or spear (pl. XLVIc).

Human worshippers, representing the seal owner, do not often appear, but on pl. XLVIb there is no reason why the bowman in a round cap should not be the prince owning the signet ring, with his name labeling his portrayal. He lifts his right fist respectfully

---

[132] For the Syrian character of the female sphinx see *AAAO*, pp. 157-158. A different view is held by J. V. Canby in *JNES* 34 (1975), pp. 225-248.

before the goddess of war and love who proffers, in return, the sign "well-being." She resembles in all respects her image at Yazilikaya (pl. XXIXc). The gold signet ring of another Hittite prince actually turned up—probably robbed from his grave—in the hands of a dealer at Konya around the beginning of this century (pl. XLVId). Once more the same goddess is shown, her half-skirt wind-blown by her swift movement. This time she rides, and holds by a rein, a sphinx that is itself divine: it has the horned pointed crown of divinity on its human head and, in addition, a lioness' head grows out of its chest.

Plate XLVIe shows a biconvex seal of the type that went on being used into the first millennium B.C.[133] While the later designs are mostly limited to hieroglyphic inscriptions, some of the early examples have a detailed divine image as their central motif. In the present instance we see the hunting god with his falcon, shouldering a crook on one face, a bow on the other.

Conclusion

In conclusion, one may be justified in stating that second-millennium Anatolia, due to its Syro-Mesopotamian contacts, underwent an amalgamation of three traditions in religion and iconography: Mesopotamia contributed its neat genealogy and hierarchy of gods with their clear-cut cosmic division of labor; Syria its colorful mythology, without morals but full of adventure stories and ingenious explanations of natural phenomena; and Anatolia the age-old reverence for its impressive geographic features, whose numina were presided by a mother-type earth and nature goddess. In the earlier second millennium direct influence from Mesopotamia and Syria was strong, but Anatolian deities—a god of violent death, a goddess of earth and nature, the hunting god, the bull of thunder—took precedence.

In the later second millennium official Anatolian religion became organized into an Olympus-like pantheon which had its origin in the Syro-Anatolian border area (the same region that so enriched Greek art and mythology in the 8th century B.C.). At the same time Anatolian iconography developed a clearly recognizable character of its own, which subsequently influenced North Syria—and ultimately Greece—in the early first millennium B.C. The thunder-and-lightning god reigned supreme, but the maternal qualities of his wife were emphasized. Her solar aspect seems not to have left much impact on later developments. On a more popular level worship of the hunting god and his nature goddess mother, be she named Iya(ya) or Kubaba, went on. First-millennium Anatolia was to witness a great revival of her popularity, with which we will deal in a later fascicle.

---

[133] D. G. Hogarth, *Hittite Seals* (Oxford, 1920), pp. 89-91.

CATALOGUE OF ILLUSTRATIONS

Plate I

a) Lead figurine group of moon god (?), wife and daughter, allegedly from Kültepe (ancient Kanesh), Turkey, *ca.* 2000-1925 B.C. Height 6.6, width 3.5 cm. Photograph courtesy Louvre Museum (no. AO 9245), Paris; see *ALF*, pl. III: 2.

b) Lead figurine of god with scimitar from Bogazköy (ancient Hattusa), Turkey, ca. 1825-1725 B.C. Height 7.4, width 1.8 cm. Ankara Archeological Museum. After *ALF*, pl. V: 6.

c) Impression of chlorite mold from Alishar, Turkey, *ca.* 1825-1725 B.C.: god with spear, wife and daughter. Height 5.7, width 3.9 cm. Ankara Archeological Museum, no. 12362. Photograph courtesy of the Oriental Institute, University of Chicago.

d) Impression of limestone mold from Bogazköy (ancient Hattusa), Turkey, *ca.* 1925-1825 B.C.: goddess with animals. Height 7.8, width 5.4 cm. Ankara Archeological Museum. After *ALF*, pl. IV: 1b.

e) Lead figurine of goddess supporting her breasts from Kültepe (ancient Kanesh), Turkey, *ca.* 1925-1825 B.C. Height 4.3, width 2.0 cm. Ankara Archeological Museum. After *ALF* p. V: 1.

Plate II

a) Chlorite mold from Kültepe (ancient Kanesh), Turkey, *ca.* 1825-1725 B.C.: god with spear and axe, wife and two daughters. Height 6.2, width 5.0 cm. Ankara Archeological Museum. Photograph Hirmer Verlag, Munich see *ALF*, pl. VI: 3.

b) Lead figurine of winged bearded god from Zincirli (ancient Samʾal), Turkey, *ca.* 1825-1725 B.C.; damage to base is recent. Height 6.4, width 4.1 cm. Photograph Berlin Vorderasiatische Museum; see *ALF*, pl. VIII: 2.

c) Lead figurine of winged, bearded god with birds from Alishar, Turkey, *ca.* 1825-1725 B.C. Height 5.6, width 4.5 cm. Ankara Archeological Museum. Photograph courtesy of the Oriental Institute, University of Chicago.

d) Impression of chlorite mold from Kültepe, (ancient Kanesh), Turkey, *ca.* 1825-1725 B.C.: winged, bearded god on four-legged pedestal. Height 7.7, width 5.2 cm. Ankara Archeological Museum. After *ALF*, pl. XV: 1.

Plate III

a) Chlorite mold from Kültepe (ancient Kanesh), Turkey, *ca.* 1825-1725 B.C.: breast-cupping goddess with son on donkey. Ankara Archeological Museum, no. 19081. After *ALF*, pl. IX: 1.

b) Lead figurine of naked goddess from Alishar, Turkey, *ca.* 1825-1725 B.C. Height 6.3, width 1.6 cm. Ankara Archeological Museum, no. 12358. Photograph courtesy of the Oriental Institute, University of Chicago.

c) Lead figurine of clothed goddess from Alishar, Turkey, *ca.* 1825-1725 B.C. Height 5.6, width 1.5 cm. Chicago, Oriental Institute. Photograph courtesy of the Oriental Institute, University of Chicago.

d) Impression of serpentine mold, allegedly from Kültepe (ancient Kanesh), Turkey, *ca.* 1825-1725 B.C.: goddess unveiling in winged gate. Istanbul, Van Aulock collection. After *ALF*, pl. XI: 4.

Plate IV

a) Lead figurine of winged goddess from Karahöyük near Konya, Turkey, *ca.* 1825-1725 B.C. Height 6.3, width *ca.* 3 cm. Karahöyük Excavations. Photograph kindly supplied by Dr. Tahsin Özgüç; see *ALF*, pp. 146-147.

b) Ivory statuette of seated goddess supporting her breasts from Kültepe (ancient Kanesh), Turkey, *ca.* 1825-1725 B.C. Height 9.3, width *ca.* 2.5 cm. Ankara Archeological Museum. Photograph Hirmer Verlag, Munich.

Plate V

a) Seal impression on clay tablet from Kültepe (ancient Kanesh), Turkey, *ca.* 1925-1825 B.C.: lightning god, steppe god, praying god, sun god before war god. Circumference of seal *ca.* 3.8, height *ca.* 2.1 cm.* Ankara Archeological Museum/Kültepe Excavation no. a/k 411. After *AG*, pl. I: 2.

b) Seal impression on clay tablet from Kültepe (ancient Kanesh), Turkey, *ca.* 1925-1825 B.C.: worshipper before water god; worshippers before bull statue. Circumference of seal ca. 4.8, height ca. 2.4 cm.* Ankara Archeological Museum/Kültepe Excavation no. a/k 494, c/k 1254, j/k 519. After *AG*, pl. V: 15.

c) Seal impression on clay tablet from Kültepe (ancient Kanesh), Turkey, *ca.* 1925-1825 B.C.: (right to left) thunder god, lightning god and praying god before war god. Circumference of seal *ca.* 7.1, height *ca.* 3.4 cm.* Ankara Archeological Museum/Kültepe Excavation no. g/k 22-23, m/k 62. After *AG*, pl. IV: 11.

Plate VI

a) Seal impression on clay tablet from Kültepe (ancient Kanesh), Turkey, *ca.* 1925-1825 B.C.: hunting god, lightning god emerging from winged gate, thunder god before altar. Circumference of seal *ca.* 8.0, height *ca.* 4.0 cm.* Ankara Archeological Museum/Kültepe Excavation no. a/k 488 etc. After *AG*, pl. VI: 17.

b) Seal impression on clay tablet from Kültepe (ancient Kanesh), Turkey, *ca.* 1925-1825 B.C.: (right to left) rain (?) goddess supporting breasts, lightning god killing bull, two-faced vizier before water god; inscription: Ennam-Ashur, son of Puzur-Ishtar. Circumference of seal *ca.* 5.4, height ca. 3.0 cm.* Ankara Archeological Museum/Kültepe Excavation no. a/k 487 etc. After *AG*, pl. VI: 18.

---

* In calculating these measurements, we have assumed all photographs in *AG* to have been printed at scale 2:1.

VII

a) Seal impression on clay tablet from Kültepe (ancient Kanesh), Turkey, *ca.* 1925-1825 B.C.: worshiper libating to lightning god; worshiper libating to god (?). Circumference of seal *ca.* 6.9, height *ca.* 3.0 cm.* Ankara Archeological Museum/Kültepe Excavation no. j/k 2. After *AG*, pl. X: 29.

b) Seal impression on clay tablet from Kültepe (ancient Kanesh), Turkey, *ca.* 1925-1825 B.C.: worshipers, back to back, before bull statue and war god, respectively. Circumference of seal *ca.* 7.7, height *ca.* 3.2 cm.* Ankara Archeological Museum/Kültepe Excavation no. f/k 180. After *AG*, pl. XIV: 40.

Plate VIII

a) Seal impression on clay tablet from Kültepe (ancient Kanesh), Turkey, *ca.* 1925-1825 B.C.: (from right) kneeling archer and spearman carrying human head on battlefield; war god surrounded by animals. Circumference of seal *ca.* 4.9, height *ca.* 2.4 cm.* Ankara Archeological Museum/Kültepe Excavation no. d/k 33. After *AG*, pl. XVII: 50.

b) Seal impression on clay tablet from Kültepe (ancient Kanesh), Turkey, *ca.* 1925-1825 B.C.: hunting god surrounded by animals and thunder god riding on bull, back to back. Circumference of seal *ca.* 8.0, height ca. 3.3 cm.* Ankara Archeological Museum/Kültepe Excavation no. a/k 305, c/k 981. After *AG*, pl. XXI: 63.

Plate IX

a) Seal impression on clay tablet from Kültepe (ancient Kanesh), Turkey, *ca.* 1925-1825 B.C.: hunting god, thunder god, lightning god emerging from winged gate and war god. Circumference of seal *ca.* 5.0, height *ca.* 2.2 cm.* Ankara Archeological Museum/Kültepe Excavation no. k/k 35. After *AG*, pl. XXII: 65.

b) Seal impression on clay tablet from Kültepe (ancient Kanesh). Turkey, *ca.* 1925-1825 B.C.: minor gods, back to back, libating to mistress of animals and war god, respectively. Circumference of seal *ca.* 4.4, height *ca.* 1.9 cm.* Ankara Archeological Museum/Kültepe Excavation no. c/k 841. After *AG*, pl. XXIV: 73.

c) Seal impression on clay tablet from Kültepe (ancient Kanesh), Turkey, *ca.* 1925-1825 B.C.: (right to left) mistress of animals, lightning god emerging from winged gate, thunder god before war god. Circumference of seal *ca.* 7.7, height ca. 3.2 cm.* Ankara Archeological Museum/Kültepe Excavation no. g/k 14. After *AG*, pl. XXIV: 71.

Plate X

a) Impression of stamp seal from Acemhöyük, Turkey, *ca.* 1800-1750 B.C.: lightning god on bull emerging from winged gate; rainbow, rain and earth (?), lizard, fish, goats, monkey. Diameter of seal *ca.* 3.8 cm. Ankara Archeological Museum/Acemhöyük Excavation no. l 1. Photograph kindly supplied by Dr. Nimet Özgüç; see same in Edith Porada, ed., *Ancient Art in Seals* (Princeton, 1980), fig. III: 24.

b) Stamp seal impression on clay from Acemhöyük, Turkey, *ca.* 1800-1750 B.C.: obelisk (?) flanked by praying goddess (?) and seated lady. Diameter of seal *ca.* 2.5 cm. Ankara Archeological Museum. Photograph kindly supplied by Dr. Nimet Özgüç.

c) Bronze figurine of smiting god from Dövlek, Turkey, *ca.* 1500 B.C. Height 11.4. cm. Ankara Archeological Museum. Photograph kindly supplied by Dr. Tahsin Özgüç.

d) Bronze figurine of god, ending in peg below, from Arapkir, Turkey, *ca.* 1500 B.C. Height 7.0 cm. Photograph courtesy University of Tübingen Institut für Vor- und Frühgeschichte.

Plate XI

a) Hematite stamp-cylinder seal, formerly in the Tyszkiewicz collection, probably from southwest Turkey, *ca.* 1700-1600 B.C., with its impressions: (center to right) lightning god dismounts from bull, while his consort (above lion) disrobes; lightning god smites enemy, corpse cremated by mourners; rain falls on man and crops; (center to left) moon god, thunder god and sun god introduced by two-faced vizier to water god. Height of seal with handle 5.8 cm, diameter 2.2 cm. Boston Museum of Fine Arts 98.706 Henry Lillie Pierce Residuary Fund. Photograph courtesy Boston Museum of Fine Arts.

b) Hematite five-faceted seal said to come from Tarsus, Turkey, *ca.* 1600-1500 B.C., with its facets: 1) worshipper before mistress of animals with kid; 2) eagle-headed genius libating before nature goddess who reaches plant; 3) god with two staffs before god with bird on trident; 4) hunting god with falcon and hare; 5) worshipper before goddess. Height of seal with handle 3.9 cm. Photograph courtesy Ashmolean Museum, Oxford.

Plate XII

a) Fragment of painted and burnished relief-decorated jar from Bitik, Turkey, ca. 1600 B.C.: (bottom to top) duel, offering bearers, wedding. Height 36.5 cm. Ankara Archeological Museum. Photograph Hirmer Verlag, Munich.

b) Painted and burnished clay bull-shaped vessels with nose rings and ropes, from Bogazköy (ancient Hattusa), Turkey, *ca.* 1600-1500 B.C. Height *ca.* 90 cm. Ankara Archeological Museum. After T. Özgüç, *Die Hethiter*, p. 3.

Plate XIII

a) Painted and relief-decorated pottery sherd from Bogazköy (ancient Hattusa), Turkey, *ca.* 1500 B.C.: musician with bull mask. Height 14.4 cm. Ankara Archeological Museum. After Bittel, *Les Hittites*, fig. 143.

b) Bronze relief-decorated vessel fragment from Bogazköy (ancient Hattusa), Turkey, 1500-1300 B.C.: young man in ''cutaway'' offers calf's-head rhyton. Height 4.5 cm. Bogazköy Museum. Bogazköy Expedition photograph.

c) Impression of hematite cylinder seal in Louvre Museum, Paris (no. AO 20138), from southeast Turkey, 1500-1400 B.C. (base has Hittite hieroglyphs); top register: victorious gods, eagle genius libating, defeated gods; bottom register: hunting god, hunting chariots. Heigh 4.5, diameter 2.2 cm. Photograph kindly supplied by P. Amiet, Louvre Museum; see same, *Bas Reliefs Imaginaires de l'Ancien Orient* (Hotel de la Monnaie exhibition catalog, Paris, 1973), no. 390.

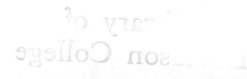

Plate XIV

a) Exterior of sphinx gate at Alaca Höyük, Turkey, toward 1300 B.C., with front view of left corner block. Height of sphinxes *ca.* 2 m. After Bossert, *Altanatolien*, fig. 497. For a reconstruction see Mellink in *Anatolia/Anadolu* 14 (1970), pp. 15-27;

b) Side view of left corner block, sphinx gate at Alaca Höyük, Turkey, toward 1300 B.C. Height 1.26 m. After Bossert, *Altanatolien*, fig. 511.

Plate XV

a) Skirt and feet of goddess on double eagle grasping hares in sphinx gate at Alaca Höyük, Turkey, toward 1300 B.C. Photograph author. For the identical left-hand door jamb, see Bittel, *Les Hittites*, frontispiece.

b) Andesite relief slab from Alaca Höyük, Turkey, toward 1300 B.C.: three priests. Height 1.33 m. Ankara Archeological Museum. Photograph Hirmer Verlag, Munich.

c) Andesite relief slab from Alaca Höyük, Turkey, toward 1300 B.C.: priest leading rams and goats. Height 1.28 m. Ankara Archeological Museum. Photograph kindly supplied by Prof. Dr. Tahsin Özgüç.

d) Andesite relief slab from Alaca Höyük, Turkey, toward 1300 B.C.: queen and king worshiping bull statue. Height 1.26 m. Ankara Archaeological Museum. Photograph Hirmer Verlag, Munich.

Plate XVI

a) Andesite relief slab from Alaca Höyük, Turkey, toward 1300 B.C.: lute player and man with monkey (?). Height 1.09 m. Ankara Archeological Museum. Photograph kindly supplied by Prof. Dr. Tahsin Özgüç.

b) Andesite relief slab from Alaca Höyük, Turkey, toward 1300 B.C.: sword eater and acrobats. Height 1.16 m. Ankara Archeological Museum. Photograph Hirmer Verlag, Munich.

c) Andesite relief slabs from Alaca Höyük, Turkey, toward 1300 B.C.: three worshipers before goddess with bowl and plant (?). Height *ca.* 1.25 m. Ankara Archeological Museum. Photograph kindly supplied by Prof. Dr. Tahsin Özgüç.

d) Andesite relief slab from Alaca Höyük, Turkey, toward 1300 B.C.: priest before lightning god. Height 1.02 m. Ankara Archeological Museum. Photograph Hirmer Verlag, Munich.

Plate XVII

a) Rock relief at Firaktin in Taurus mountains, Turkey, 1275-1250 B.C.: king Hattusili III libating before god with crook, queen Puduhepa libating before goddess with bird. Width *ca.* 3.25, height *ca.* 1.30 m. Photograph kindly supplied by Dr. Hatice Gonnet.

b) Stone altar with inscription of Tudhaliya IV from Eski Kişla near Emirgazi east of Konya, 1250-1225 B.C. Height *ca.* 90, diameter 50 cm. Istanbul Archeological Museum no. 7770. After B. Hrozny, *Les inscriptions hittites hiéroglyphiques* I:3 (Prague, 1937), pl. 78.

c) Rock relief at Imamkulu in Taurus mountains, Turkey, 1300-1200 B.C.: thunder god riding on bull chariot over backs of three mountain gods supported by three eagle genii. Heigth *ca.* 2 m. After M. Wäfler in *MDOG* 107 (1975), pl. 3.

Plate XVIII

a) Rock niche with relief figure in pointed cap holding bow and staff at Karabel near Izmir, Turkey, 1250-1200 B.C. Height 2.32 m. Photograph Hirmer Verlag, Munich.

b) Rock niche with frontal seated goddess (?) carved in high relief at Akpinar near Manisa, western Turkey, 1300-1200 B.C. Height *ca.* 9 m. Photograph Hirmer Verlag, Munich.

Plate XIX

a) Rock relief on hill-top mausoleum (?) at Gâvur Kalesi southwest of Ankara, Turkey, 1300-1200 B.C.: (from right) bearded god and beardless god greeting seated deity with bowl at far left. Height *ca.* 3.50 m. Photograph Hirmer Verlag, Munich.

b) Stone relief stele from Akçaköy west of Cerablus, southeast Turkey, 1400-1200 B.C.: lightning god with spear. Height 1.40 m. Adana Archeological Museum. After Bossert, *Altanatolien*, fig. 567.

c) Limestone relief block found near temple I at Bogazköy (ancient Hattusa), Turkey, 1400-1300 B.C.: prince in kilt and shawl before wickerwork altar. Height 0.67 m. Istanbul Archeological Museum. Photograph Hirmer Verlag, Munich.

Plate XX

Temple I or temple of storm god and sun goddess surrounded by its storerooms at Bogazköy (ancient Hattusa), Turkey, 1275-1250 B.C.: priests' quarters in background (facing southwest). Width *ca.* 130, depth *ca.* 200 m. After *MDOG* 101 (1969), fig. 2.

Plate XXI

Temple of storm god and sun goddess at Bogazköy (ancient Hattusa), Turkey, 1275-1250 B.C. (facing northeast). Width *ca.* 45, depth *ca.* 65 m. Photograph author.

Plate XXII

Southeast cella in temple of storm god and sun goddess at Bogazköy (ancient Hattusa), Turkey, 1275-1250 B.C. (facing northeast). Width *ca.* 8, depth *ca.* 11 m. Photograph author.

Plate XXIII

Temple II (right) and III (left) in upper city at Bogazköy (ancient Hattusa), Turkey, 1300-1200 B.C. (facing north). Sizes *ca.* 47 × 35, 55 × 38 m. Photograph Hirmer Verlag, Munich.

Plate XXIV

Limestone outer jamb of 'royal gate' in city wall at Bogazköy (ancient Hattusa), Turkey, 1400-1200 B.C.: god with battle axe. Height 2.25 m. Ankara Archeological Museum. Photograph Hirmer Verlag, Munich.

Plate XXV

Main chamber (chamber A) of open-air sanctuary with rock reliefs at Yazilikaya near Bogazköy (ancient Hattusa), Turkey, *ca.* 1250 B.C. Depth 18 m. Width 13 m. Photograph Hirmer Verlag, München; see *HFY*, pl. 8:2.

Plate XXVI

a) Twelve warrior gods and mountain god (figures 1-13 in the procession of gods), rock relief in chamber A at Yazilikaya near Bogazköy (ancient Hattusa), Turkey, *ca.* 1250 B.C. Width *ca.* 4.50, height *ca.* 0.85 m. After *HFY*, pl. 12:1.

b) Two mountain gods with bent caps and two young gods, one armed with mace (figures 16a-19 in the procession of gods), rock relief in chamber A at Yazilikaya, *ca.* 1250 B.C. Width *ca.* 1.50, height 0.70-0.75 m, with bench for offerings in front. After *HFY*, pl. 15:2.

Plate XXVII

a) Three young and two older gods (figures 20-24 in the procession of gods), rock relief in chamber A at Yazilikaya, ca. 1250 B.C. Width *ca.* 2.50, height *ca.* 0.75 m, with bench for offerings in front. After *HFY*, pl. 16:1.

b) God Pisaisaphi and god of the Netherworld, both armed with scimitars; bull-men Seri and Hurri keeping heaven and earth apart (figures 26-29 in the procession of gods), rock relief in chamber A at Yazilikaya, *ca.* 1250 B.C. Width *ca.* 2, height 0.75-1 m, with bench for offerings in front. Photograph Hirmer Verlag, München; see *HFY*, pl. 19:1.

Plate XXVIII

a) War god Hesue (figure 30 in the procession of gods), rock relief in chamber A at Yazilikaya, *ca.* 1250 B.C. Width *ca.* 0.50, height *ca.* 0.80 m. After *HFY*, pl. 20:2.

b) Winged deity Pirinkar (figure 31 in the procession of gods), rock relief in chamber A at Yazilikaya, *ca.* 1250 B.C. Width *ca.* 0.50, height *ca.* 0.75 m. After *HFY*, pl. 20:3.

c) Figures 25-31 (see above), protective god Nubadig (?) and war god Astabi (figures 32-33 in the procession of gods), rock relief in chamber A at Yazilikaya, *ca.* 1250 B.C. Width *ca.* 1, height ca. 0.80 m. Photograph author.

Plate XXIX

a) Sun god Simegi, moon god Kusuh, Sauska with her retinue, and water god Ea (figures 34-39 in the procession of gods), rock relief in chamber A at Yazilikaya, *ca.* 1250 B.C. Width *ca.* 4.75, height *ca.* 0.85 m, with rock-cut bench, drain and basin for libations. After *HFY*, pl. 23:1.

b) Kulitta and Ninatta, handmaidens on the deity of war and love (figures 36-37 in the procession of gods), rock relief in chamber A at Yazilikaya, *ca.* 1225 B.C. Width *ca.* 1, height *ca.* 0.85 m. Photograph (of cast) Hirmer Verlag, München; see *HFY*, pl. 22:4.

c) Sauska, deity of war and love, dawn and dusk in her martial aspect (figure 38 in the procession of gods), rock relief in chamber A at Yazilikaya, *ca.* 1250 B.C. Width *ca.* 0.50, height *ca.* 0.90 m. Photograph (of cast) Hirmer Verlag, München; see *HFY*, pl. 23:2.

Plate XXX

Lightning god Tesub, with his calf on two mountain gods, greeting his wife Hebat, with her calf on a lioness: figures 42-43 of the rock relief in chamber A at Yazilikaya, *ca.* 1250 B.C. Width *ca.* 2, height *ca.* 2.50 m. After *HFY*, pl. 28.

Plate XXXI

Main scene (figures 41-46) of the rock relief in chamber A at Yazilikaya, *ca.* 1250 B.C. Behind Hebat (cf. pl. XXX) are her son Sarruma on a lion cub, her daughter Alanzu and her grand-daughter on a double eagle. Width *ca.* 5, height *ca.* 2.50 m. Photograph Hirmer Verlag. München; see *HFY*, pl. 26:1.

Plate XXXII

a) Grain god Kumarbi (figure 40 in the procession of gods), rock relief in chamber A at Yazilikaya, *ca.* 1250 B.C. Width *ca.* 0.50, height *ca.* 2.20 m. After *HFY*, pl. 24:2.

b) Probably Tasmisu, brother of the storm god (figure 41 in the procession of gods), rock relief in chamber A at Yazilikaya, *ca.* 1250 B.C. Width *ca.* 0.75, height *ca.* 2.30 m; god's figure only 1.50 m high. After *HFY*, pl. 24:3.

c) Goddess that must have preceded Sauska, deity of war and love, dawn and dusk in her amatory aspect: relief found at Yekbas near Bogazköy, which may have fitted with two or three others between figures 46 and 46a of the rock relief in chamber A at Yazilikaya, *ca.* 1250 B.C. Width *ca.* 0.65, height *ca.* 0.90 m. After *HFY*, pl. 36:3.

d) Goddess representing the Hutellura (figure 48 in the procession of gods), rock relief in chamber A at Yazilikaya, *ca.* 1250 B.C. Width *ca.* 0.50, height *ca.* 0.80 m. After *HFY*, pl. 32:4.

Plate XXXIII

a) Three unknown goddesses, Tapkina, Nikkal and Aya (figures 50-55 in the procession of gods), rock relief in chamber A at Yazilikaya, *ca.* 1250 B.C. Width *ca.* 3.50, height *ca.* 0.80 m, with rock-cut pillar for placing offerings. Photograph Hirmer Verlag, München; see *HFY*, pl. 36:1.

b) Twelve warrior gods (figures 69-80 in chamber B), rock relief at Yazilikaya, *ca.* 1225 B.C. Width *ca.* 2.85, height *ca.* 0.80 m. After *HFY*, pl. 45:1.

Plate XXXIV

King Tudhaliya IV on two mountains, greeting the gods (figure 64 in chamber A), rock relief at Yazilikaya, *ca.* 1225 B.C. Width *ca.* 2.20, height *ca.* 2.95 m. After *HFY*, pl. 39:2.

Plate XXXV

God Sarruma protecting King Tudhaliya IV, rock relief 81 in chamber B at Yazilikaya, *ca.* 1225 B.C. Width *ca.* 1.40, height *ca.* 1.60 m. Photograph Hirmer Verlag, München; see *HFY*, pl. VII.

Plate XXXVI

Same as preceding, cast taken before damage to king's face. Photograph Hirmer Verlag, München; see *HFY*, pl. 49.

Plate XXXVII

God of the Netherworld, with body shaped like sword stuck into ground, rock relief 82 in chamber B at Yazilikaya, *ca.* 1225 B.C. Width *ca.* 1.10, height *ca.* 3.40 m. Photograph Hirmer Verlag, München; see *HFY*, pl. 51.

Plate XXXVIII

Unfinished limestone stela at Fasillar southeast of lake Beyşehir, Turkey, *ca.* 1200 B.C.: smiting god on mountain god flanked by lions. Height 7.40 m. Cast in Ankara Archeological Museum. Photograph by author of cast in Ankara Museum.

Plate XXXIX

Dry stone monument at Eflâtun Pinar east of lake Beyşehir, Turkey, toward 1200 B.C.: divine couple seated under triple winged disk held up by genii. Width 7.10, height 4.20 m. Photograph Hirmer Verlag, Munich.

Plate XL

a) Silver cup in shape of kneeling stag in Norbert Schimmel Collection, New York, from Turkey, *ca.* 1400 B.C. Height 18 cm. Photograph kindly supplied by the owner.

b) Embossed and engraved scene on rim of silver cup in shape of kneeling stag (see pl. XLa): (from right) stag hunters worship hunting god and his mother. After Muscarella, *Ancient Art*, no. 123.

c) Silver cup in shape of kneeling bull in Norbert Schimmel Collection, New York, from Turkey, 1400-1300 B.C. Height 18 cm. Photograph kindly supplied by the owner.

d) Gold pendant figurine of mother goddess with baby on her lap in Norbert Schimmel Collection, New York, from Turkey, 1300-1200 B.C. Height 4.3 cm. Photograph kindly supplied by the owner.

Plate XLI

a) Gold pendant figurine of beardless god with staff, from Yozgat, Turkey, 1400-1200 B.C. Height 2.5 cm. London, British Museum. Photograph British Museum.

b) Gold pendant figurine of seated goddess holding bowl, from Bogazköy (ancient Hattusa), Turkey, 1400-1200 B.C. Height 2.0 cm. Ankara Archeological Museum. Photograph Hirmer Verlag, Munich.

c) Silver pendant figurine of bull from Bogazköy (ancient Hattusa), Turkey, 1300-1200 B.C. Height 2.7 cm. Ankara Archeological Museum. Photograph kindly supplied by Prof. Dr. Tahsin Özgüç.

d) Ivory figurine of mountain god from Bogazköy (ancient Hattusa), Turkey, 1300-1200 B.C. Height 3.6 cm. Ankara Archeological Museum. Photograph Hirmer Verlag, Munich.

Plate XLII

a) Electrum pendant figurine of priest (?) with bull mask flanked by gods (?) with crooks, from Ras Shamra (ancient Ugarit), Syria, 1400-1300 B.C. Height *ca.* 3 cm. Private collection. After *Ugaritica III*, fig. 114.

b) Steatite miniature relief stela from Yeniköy near Alaca Höyük, Turkey, 1400-1200 B.C.: hunting god with crook and falcon on stag. Height 6.3 cm. Ankara Archeological Museum. Photograph Hirmer Verlag, Munich.

c) Bronze miniature stela with relief base from Alaca Höyük, Turkey, 1400-1300 B.C.: winged sun disk on tree supported by bull-men on bulls. Height 14.5 cm. Ankara Archeological Museum. Photograph Hirmer Verlag, Munich.

d) Gold embossed disk said to come from Izmir, Turkey, 1400-1300 B.C.: winged sun disks on trees supported by bull-men; lions, bulls and trees; human heads. Diameter 19.7 cm. Chicago, Oriental Institute. Photograph courtesy Oriental Institute.

Plate XLIII

a) Bronze statuette of smiting (?) god from Dogantepe (Zara) near Amasya, Turkey, toward 1300 B.C. Height 21.5 cm. Amasya, Bayezid Külliyesi. After *Der Alte Orient*, fig. 334b.

b) Bronze statuette of marching god from Bogazköy (ancient Hattusa), Turkey, 1400-1200 B.C. Height 14.7 cm. Berlin, Staatliche Museen. After Akurgal, *Kunst der Hethiter*, pl. 51.

c) Bronze statuette of marching god from Latakia, Syria, 1400-1200 B.C. Height 15.3 cm. Paris, Louvre Museum. Photograph kindly supplied by P. Amiet.

Plate XLIV

a) Lapis lazuli inlay figure in gold setting from Cerablus (ancient Carchemish), Turkey, *ca.* 1200 B.C.: hunting god with bow and falcon. Height 1.3 cm. London, British Museum. Photograph Hirmer Verlag, Munich.

b) Lapis lazuli inlay figure of hunting god with throwing stick, falcon and hare, from Qalᶜat Shergat (ancient Assur), Iraq, 1400-1250 B.C. Height 2.2 cm. Berlin, Staatliche Museen. Photograph Staatliche Museen.

c) Gold inlay figure of sun god with crook and 'life' sign from Cerablus (ancient Carchemish), Turkey, *ca.* 1200 B.C. Height 1.7 cm. London, British Museum. Photograph Hirmer Verlag, Munich.

d) Additional lapis lazuli and gold inlay figures from the same group as pl. XLIVa, c: god with bow, god with bow and spear, winged goddess, kneeling eagle genius; moon god, winged goddess, young god, goddess. Height 1.4-1.7 cm. Photograph British Museum.

Plate XLV

a) Seal impression on clay from Bogazköy (ancient Hattusa), Turkey, *ca.* 1300 B.C.: great king (emperor) Muwattali protected by the great storm god of heaven. Diameter 5.6 cm. Ankara Archeological Museum. After T. Özgüç, *Die Hethiter*, p. 36.

b) Seal impression on clay of great king Tudhaliya IV from Ras Shamra (ancient Ugarit), Syria, *ca.* 1225 B.C.: sun goddess and storm god with their son Sarruma. Diameter 5.5 cm. Damascus National Museum. After *Ugaritica* III, fig. 26.

c) Stamp seal impression on clay of Ini-Tesub, king of Carchemish, from Ras Shamra (ancient Ugarit), Syria, *ca.* 1250 B.C.: lightning god with sphinx on fist. Diameter 4.6 cm. Damascus National Museum. After *Ugaritica* III, fig. 28.

d) Impression on clay of second seal of great king Tudhaliya IV from Bogazköy (ancient Hattusa), Turkey, *ca.* 1225 B.C.: mountain god Tudhaliya with mace and 'well-being' sign. Height *ca.* 3.7 cm. Ankara Archaeological Museum. Photograph kindly supplied by prof. Dr. Tahsin Özgüç.

Plate XLVI

a) Cylinder seal impression on clay of Ini-Tesub, king of Carchemish, from Ras Shamra (ancient Ugarit), Syria, *ca.* 1250 B.C.: calf on mountain, lightning god on two mountain gods, Sarruma on eagle genius, thunder god (?) on bull fighting lion. Circumference of seal *ca.* 4.7 cm. Damascus National Museum. After *Ugaritica* III, fig. 33.

b) Signet ring impression on clay of prince Taki-Sarruma from Ras Shamra (ancient Ugarit), Syria, *ca.* 1250 B.C.: war and love goddess proffering 'well-being' sign to prince with bow. Height of ring *ca.* 1.3 cm. Damascus National Museum. After *Ugaritica* III, fig. 56.

c) Cylinder seal impression on clay of Amanmasu from Ras Shamra (ancient Ugarit), Syria, *ca.* 1250 B.C.: lightning god on two mountain gods, sun god on lion, Sarruma on eagle genius. Circumference of seal 4.5 cm. Damascus National Museum. After *Ugaritica* III, fig. 67.

d) Gold signet ring of prince 'Great Lion' from Konya, Turkey, *ca.* 1250 B.C.: war and love goddess proffering 'well-being' sign and riding two-headed sphinx. Height of ring 1.3 cm. Oxford, Ashmolean Museum. Photograph courtesy Ashmolean Museum.

e) Chlorite two-faced stamp seal from Tel Beşir near Gaziantep, Turkey, toward 1200 B.C.: hunting god with crook and falcon; hunting god with bow and falcon. Diameter 3.1 cm. Oxford, Ashmolean Museum. Photograph courtesy Ashmolean Museum.

PLATES I-XLVI

a) Kültepe triad   b) **Bogazköy god**

c) Alishar triad   d) **Bogazköy goddess**   e) Kültepe goddess

Plate II   *Lead figurines and molds, 1825-1725*

a) Kültepe family

b) Zincirli god

c) Alishar god

d) Kültepe god

a) Kültepe goddess with son

b) Alishar
naked
goddess

c) Alishar clothed
goddess

d) Kültepe disrobing goddess

Plate IV　　　　　*Lead and ivory figurines, 1825-1725*

a) Karahöyük naked goddess　　　　　b) Kültepe naked goddess

a) Gods before war god

b) Worshippers before water god, bull statue

c) Gods before war god

a) Three gods, altar

b) Gods before water god

a) Worshippers libating to gods

b) Worshippers before bull statue, war god

Plate VIII   *Seal impressions from Kültepe, 1925-1825*

a) War god and helpers

b) Hunting god and thunder god

a) Gods on mounts

b) Libations to mistress of animals, war god

c) War god, gods on mounts, mistress of animals

Plate X *Seal impressions, 1800-1750; bronze figurines, ca. 1500 B.C.*

a) Acemhöyük god with rainbow

b) Acemhöyük obelisk worship

c) Dövlek smiting god

d) Arapkir peg god

Hematite hammer seals, 1700-1500   *Plate XI*

a) Boston Museum of Fine Arts: water god, smiting god

b) Tarsus (?): nature goddesses and gods

Plate XII   *Painted vessels, 1600-1500*

a) Bitik jar: temple (?) feast

b) Bogazköy bull vessels

a) Bogazköy musician with mask

b) Bogazköy man with calf's head

c) Southeast Turkey (?): victorious gods, hunting charioteers

Plate XIV   *Alaca Höyük gate, toward 1300 B.C.*

a) Exterior of sphinx gate, with front view of left corner block

b) Side view of left corner block

b) Three priests

d) Queen, king worshiping bull

a) Double eagle with hares

c) Priest with rams and goats

b) Acrobats

a) Musicians

a) Firaktin: libations to hunting deities

b) Emirgazi: altar inscribed by
Tudhaliya IV

c) Imamkulu: prince, storm god

Plate XVIII *Rock reliefs in western Turkey, 1300-1200*

b) Akpinar: frontal goddess (?)

a) Gâvur Kalesi: greeting gods

b) Akçaköy: lightning god

c) Bogazköy: prince before stelae

Plate XX   *Temple I at Bogazköy, 1275-1250*

Foreground: temple, storerooms; background: priests' quarters

Temple proper, facing northeast

Plate XXII   *Temple I at Bogazköy, 1275-1250*

Temples II (right) and III (left)

Helmeted god with axe

Main chamber, facing north

a) Twelve marching gods, mountain god

b) Two mountain gods, two young gods

a) Three young gods, two older gods

b) Gods with scimitars, bull-men with heaven and earth

a) Second war god   b) Winged deity

c) (Far right) protective god and first war god

a) Sun god, moon god, war god(dess) with retinue, water god

b) Handmaidens of war god(dess)   c) War god(dess)

Lightning god on mountain gods, his wife on lioness

Supreme god with brother, wife, son, daugther and granddaughter

Plate XXXII Yazilikaya reliefs 40, 41, 48 and (c) Yekbas relief, ca. 1250 B.C.

a) Grain god

b) Lightning god's brother

c) Goddess; love goddess' name

d) Fate goddess

a) Goddesses including (right) water, moon and sun gods' wives

b) Twelve gods with scimitars

Plate XXXIV   *Yazilikaya relief 64, ca. 1225 B.C.*

King Tudhaliya IV on mountains

Supreme god's son protecting king Tudhaliya IV

Supreme god's son protecting king Tudhaliya IV (cast)

God of the nether world

Smiting god on mountain god between lions

Seated god and goddess, bull-men holding up triple winged disk

Plate XL   *Schimmel Collection silver cups, gold figurine, 1400-1200*

a) Kneeling stag

c) Kneeling bull

b) Scene on rim of (a)

d) Mother goddess

b) Bogazköy seated figure with bowl

a) Yozgat god with staff

c) Bogazköy humped bull

d) Bogazköy mountain god

a) Ras Shamra triad

b) Yeniköy hunting god

c) Alaca Höyük bull-men

d) Izmir (?) bull-men, lions, bulls, heads

c) Latakia young god

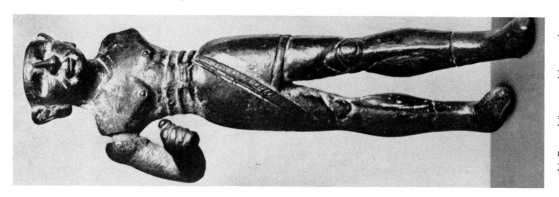

b) Bogazköy marching god

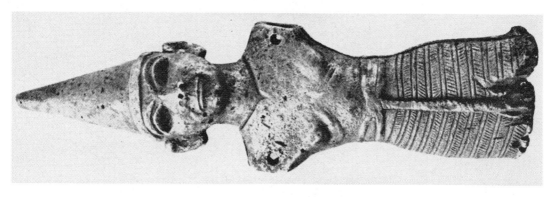

a) Dogantepe smiting god

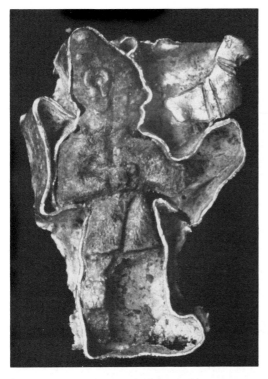

a) Cerablus hunting god

c) Cerablus sun god

b) Qal'at
Shergat hunting
god

d) Cerablus eight figures

a) Storm god protecting king

b) Storm god with family

c) Storm god with sphinx

d) Mountain god

b) War goddess with prince

d) War goddess on sphinx

e) Hunting god (twice)

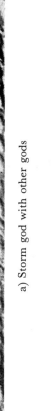

a) Storm god with other gods

c) Storm god with sun god